****

FOR WOMEN ONLY:

HOW TO

CONTROL A MAN

****

By

Harrison Forrest

Foreword by

Dr. Jack Sitoffsky

****

Sabra int'l
home for Amingway Publishing
Coral Springs, Florida

For women only: How to control a man
By Harrison Forrest
Foreword by Dr. Jack Sitoffsky

Published by:

SABRA INT'L
HOME FOR AMINGWAY PUBLISHING
POST OFFICE BOX 770546
CORAL SPRINGS, FL 33077 U.S.A.
PH:954-346-8588   FAX:954-346-6762
E-MAIL:sabra-tifferent-53@worldnet.att.net

****

Copyright c1988/1997 Sabra c/o Amingway publishing

All rights reserved. No parts of this book may be reproduced in any form without permission from the publisher, **except by a reviewer** who may quote brief passages in a review to be printed in a magazine newspaper or by radio announcement.

Cover Design:Shlomo Cohen (Seapen)

ISBN 0-9661304-0-5

Printed in the U.S.A.

10 9 8 7 6 5 4 3 2 1

CONTENTS (A)

CONTENTS (B)

****

APPENDIX

ABOUT THE AUTHOR

Harrison Forrest was born outside the United States of European parents. From a young age, he displayed an interest and fascination in the workings of the relationships between men and women. After completing service in the army, Harrison took a position with a major airline which required frequent and lengthy travel all over Europe and the Middle East.

While in this job, Harrison was a lonely wolf exploring the social world in many cities from various angles. He started doing private research involving hundreds of male participants questioning their experiences in their relationships with women. The further he became involved in this research, the more questions came to the surface.

In 1988, Harrison moved to southern Florida. Three years later, he met his lovely wife Lila Savoir. Lila brought two children and Harrison brought three children to the marriage. Lila was surrounded by many single female friends calling themselves "the sisterhood". These friends, along with their female acquaintances, became friendly with Harrison as well and began to share many of the problems they were having with men in and out of relationships.

At the time Harrison had moved to Florida, he had already written much of a book giving advice on relationships based upon his previous research and experience. The material gleaned from this book enabled him to give much advice to these women, which they found to be extremely helpful.

This group put a great deal of pressure on Harrison to complete the book, and made the suggestion that he direct it towards women. The book was born.

FOREWORD

by Dr. Jack Sitoffsky

There are a multitude of books, articles and how-to guides about male-female relationships. However, Harrison Forrest in this book has tackled a psychologically complicated topic, i.e., control, and managed to simplify a complex idea.

My initial feelings upon reading the title, were of concern; of course, I would be resistant to the idea of control. But, after reading the first few chapters, especially those regarding the nature of man and his hidden child, I realized that Forrest's approach is actually constructive and positive - one which aims to promote shared and intimate experiences. On a conscious level, a man does not know that he is being controlled; unconsciously, he's yearning for it, and the bonding which occurs.

This book dares to explore where other books have not even ventured. Although written for women, it is also appropriate and instructional for men. In a somewhat jocular but actually serious vein, Mr. Forrest discusses man's best friend and how a woman should address this little (or big) fellow. He also explains the classifications of body type preferences as well as the problems and possible solutions surrounding wrong choices for a woman.

His anecdotal stories are written with charm and humor. When a woman learns to appreciate the mystery of a man's psyche, then she can begin to enjoy a positive relationship and, in turn, a creative future with her partner.

At no time in history have there been so many restless and questioning women who are looking for ways to develop and nurture a long term relationship. "How To Control A Man" gives answers to these questions by defining salient issues, and then attempts to construct a framework for the woman to develop and work her magic.

"How To Control A Man" forthrightly confronts outdated modes of thinking and attempts to provide a modern framework for a woman to attain the heights of pleasure, love and spirituality with her man.

Jack Sitoffsky, M.D.

WHAT OTHER WOMEN ARE SAYING ABOUT THIS BOOK:

Sandra Schreiber: "After reading this book, I discovered, after all these years, that my husband is a leg man. Knowing this, I can provide a fresh approach to our relationship. The chapter on the man-child was so true to form. You will never think of ice cream the same way again!"

Fran Sloane(a member of the sisterhood): "I wish I had received a copy of this book when I got my divorce degree! It's like having a good male friend answering all my questions about men's behavior.

Bobbi Roberts(a member of the sisterhood): "I was very surprised by the depth of information and level of honesty provided in this book. It is obvious that the writer did not try to hide sensitive issues; in fact, he even emphasized them. This book is very different. On the one hand, the serious message contained within leads the reader to further thinking on the issues discussed. On the other hand, the sometimes jovial approach to several topics creates a feeling of warm fuzziness. The fact that this book was written by a man of great knowledge and experience with relationships, makes it all the more unique. Every woman should keep this book by her side as an available reference to all situations involving men."

Jennifer Alston: "As a twenty-five year old woman, it will take me a long time to digest what I found in this book. However, I am grateful to have learned so much from this book at such an early stage of my life. I have seen so many problems encountered by my divorced mother and her friends in their relationships with men. The "Red Light" chapter is a must for every woman, especially those women who are in-between relationships. I feel incredibly better having this knowledge in hand. You can be sure that I will reread this book many times over the years. Thank you Mr. Forrest."

WHAT MEN ARE SAYING ABOUT THIS BOOK:

Alex Marston: "Upon first seeing the title of this book, fear crept into my being. I could not believe that another man would advise women on methods of controlling men. However, after beginning to read the book, albeit with mixed feelings, I discovered that I would like to be the recipient of this method of control. I still don't like the idea that so many secrets about men are revealed, but the end purpose of revealing them - to educate women to create a more positive relationship with men - is to my benefit, as well as the benefit of all men."

C.J.: "I am a married man of many years experiencing an unhappy marriage. I have refused to include my name here in fear of my wife's reaction. A female friend told me about this book and, after much hesitation, I agreed to read it. On the surface, the book appears threatening to men. However, I discovered the opposite to be true, and now I will do anything to get it in my wife's hands. The ideas around "punishments" and "negative control" particularly apply in my situation. I hope that my wife will open her eyes."

ACKNOWLEDGMENTS (A)

Written words cannot describe my deep appreciation and esteem for my sweet wife, Lila Savoir, whose wisdom, kindness, patience and love have helped to lift this complicated project high up. Without sweet Lila, this book could never have been completed.

With her great talent in language, translation, and knowledge of literary form, Lila did the translation, editing, type setting, and printing preparation. I am eternally grateful to her.

Lila is the one that I love to be controlled by. I am so lucky to have her/

I am grateful to Sandi Liever, who has put her enthusiasm and effort into supporting the writing of this book.

Many thanks to Barbara Shore, who, by taking time from her busy life, contributed her knowledge and her experience to the review of this book, along with her ever-steady cheerfulness and support.

Deep appreciation goes to Bobbi Pugliese who has taken the time from her career to comment and review this book.

X

ACKNOWLEDGMENTS (B)

I am grateful to Schlomo Cohen, cartoonist, graphic designer, and artist for his contribution of the cover for this book, and for his guidance and advice based upon his many years of experience in the book industry.

Asher Diem, who has acted as assistant editor to Lila, has brought his deep knowledge of computers and previous editing experience to this project, without which we could not have completed this book in a timely fashion. We are eternally grateful to Asher, who has also contributed his long-term support and encouragement all the way.

Special thanks to Kathleen Gleason and Kevin Bristow from *Cosmopolitan* magazine, who have given their professional advice in the promotion of this book

****

WARNING-DISCLAIMER

All names appearing in the anecdotes or stories in this book are fictional and have no connection to any real person, past or present.

This book is based on two major sources: (1) private research by the writer and his assistants, involving hundreds of men on an anonymous basis; and (2) the personal experience of the writer.

The research involving the men took place in many countries. Due to its anonymous nature, the information provided by these men is intimate and to the point, without any barriers.

This book does not involve official research through any institution or scientific database. The writer was not employed by any institution during the writing of this book.

Throughout this book, any time reference is made to a particular group, the reference is to a majority population. There are always people who do not fit into a particular group, who are part of a select minority, and this book does not attempt to address them.

This book is not the ultimate answer to the problems confronted within its pages.

This book represents suggestion only and is not a holy touchstone.

CHAPTER ONE: WHY CONTROL
MAN?

The word "control" is a very strong one, and may be misconstrued in this context as having the meaning of "domination" of woman over man. In the dictionary, a number of definitions and synonyms are assigned to this word, of which "domination"is but one. The words govern, manage, rule, regulate are some other words having similar meaning. When used here, we may think of the word "manage" as being the most similar.

Yet, even so, many readers may pose the question: "Why should anyone control another person in a relationship? Shouldn't there be an equal balance of power in a relationship?"

Equability of control is the ideal situation, if at all possible. But, in reality, this concept is naive since it works only for those who have reached a high level of understanding of human nature and the opposite sex, and only where both parties in the relationship have reached this level.

For most relationships then, the best solution is to have one partner manage the other and the relationship in such a clever and pleasant manner that harmony, peace, and positive energy will result. My belief is that the woman should be the partner in control, and this book explains why.

There are many positive outcomes to a woman's control over a man. This control involves a situation wherein the woman gets what she wants in the end, **and, strangely enough, the man does not even realize it. Also, more strangely, if he will come to realize it, he will not even care.**

Generally speaking, a women's nature is endowed with great passion, love and sensitivity as compared to that of man's. Women embrace the practice of creating a more beautiful world.This is seen in their constant attempts to beautify their homes with flowers, pictures, attractive furnishings and accessories inside, and lovely gardens on the outside. In view of this, it is so sad to see how our world is still primarily controlled by men.

Why is it like this? How is it that women allow these men to assume these positions of control? If women could assume these positions, there would be less of a problem due to an inflated ego.

The basic answer always appears in the same shape and form, which is that **most women do not understand the nature of man,** his primitive secrets, his animal needs, and his basic nature. **That is why they cannot control him.** This is why there are so many **problems in the relationships** in our society which affect the whole world later on.

In general, the average man would be more than happy to be controlled by a woman who understands the pathways and byways to her man. The right way to control the man is the way of **positive control**, and realizing that there are two approaches to control:

(1) The Positive Control
(2) The Negative Control

NEGATIVE CONTROL

Unfortunately, **most women** in our world are trying to control their men through the use of **negative control.** The main reason for this situation, as I have mentioned before, is lack of knowledge or lack of understanding regarding the nature of man.

In most cases, negative control lasts for a short period of time. Following the demise of this control, an explosive condition may occur. But, if for some reason, negative control should be of a longer lasting nature, the explosion may be so severe that the situation can even end in tragedy.

An example of negative control can be seen with the parent who physically abuses his child, screams at him, and then expects him to react agreeably. However, this negative control creates inside the man a great rebelliousness, even though on the **surface** he may appear to be very calm.

So what exactly is negative control, and how does it display itself in everyday life?

As has been mentioned before, negative control is the wrong way of control and, at the end of the story, there will be **failure.**   Negative control reveals itself through screaming at the man, complaining and whining, punishing the man, and creating humiliation by laughing at the man, etc.   The pressure on the man is very heavy and lasts continuously throughout the day.   Sometimes this pressure is even applied further through remote control (e.g. telephone calls, faxes, etc.).   More examples of this negative control will appear throughout the book.

POSITIVE CONTROL

The exertion of positive control is the **best way to control the man,** yet this course is utilized by only a **few women** in our society.   These women have a high level of consciousness of the nature of men, and they take advantage of this situation for their own benefit.   These women are on the top of the pyramid, **and they can get everything they want from their men.**   They are practicing control in an intelligent manner, playing the game by understanding man's **basic needs.**

In the method of positive control, as has been mentioned previously, **the man cannot see that he is under control at all.**   And, basically, he is enjoying the ride all the way. He feels comfortable, happy, and delighted with the situation.   He will be more than happy to be with the woman who controls him in this positive way.

In order to control your man, you must understand his nature, his weak points, his dreams, his loves, and, most of all, his soul.

CHAPTER TWO: THE NATURE OF MAN AND HIS BEHAVIOR

There is a great similarity between the male human being and the male lion. In the world of the lion, the male lion's role is as the fighter, the protector, and the stud. These are his only duties throughout his lifetime.

The female lion's role is to nurture and educate the young and to hunt as part of a group. Sometimes, but very rarely, you can observe a male lion watching the young. But, most of the time, his job as protector of the pride involves his pacing back and forth over his territory, urinating constantly to mark the borders.

Although his responsibilities seem as though they would take up much time, the male lion spends most of his 24 hour day napping and playing. **I EMPHASIZE: NAPPING AND PLAYING**. The best example of this aspect of the male lion's life is exemplified by the behavior of the dolphins.

Dolphins spend more time playing than any other mammal. They are extremely intelligent animals, so, one can say that the more intelligent the animal, the stronger the desire to play. **I EMPHASIZE: THE MORE INTELLIGENT THE ANIMAL, THE GREATER THE DESIRE TO PLAY.**

If you will take a look at the children playing in your neighborhood and the dolphins at play on the one hand, and, on the other hand take a look at your man, you will see a common bond amongst all of them. This commonality is the soul of a child. **I EMPHASIZE: THE SOUL OF A CHILD.**

Basically, you have heard many ideas or theories about this issue. However, none of them have indicated what the real meaning is of the child within the man, and how this really affects his everyday behavior, his behavior towards you, and your behavior towards him. **I EMPHASIZE: YOUR BEHAVIOR TOWARDS HIM.**

So, as you can see, your man is camouflaging a child's soul. And, because of this concept, **your man is behaving in a way that you will never ever understand.**

Most of the women in our society measure a man by the sum of his outward appearances -- both physical and material, and by his financial and social position. **Everything here is camouflage.** This is a camouflage so great that there is none better by comparison. You must understand that behind this curtain of hair style, muscle, position, seriousness, self-centeredness, dress, and ego, stands hidden the soul of a child. **I EMPHASIZE: HIDDEN**

This child within carries fears, desires, need for security, need for love and compassion. **Only a smart, sensitive woman can control this child with wisdom, with touching, with slyness, and with love.**

At this point, I would like to mention that whatever is expressed in this book applies to the normal man. I know that many women will shake their heads and disagree with many of the statements in this book. But, I want to make clear that this book applies to the majority of men who still have a conscience and a heart still open towards love.(the man that is defined herein as the "normal man")

Do not think that it is impossible to find such a man, as these men are definitely out there. They may be hidden or difficult to find, but they are still out there.

In the chapter where "Red Lights" and the "Pyramid Law" are discussed, you can find information on how to locate these men.

****

CHAPTER THREE: PUNISHMENTS

A woman who wants to control her man in a positive manner, must understand that, after a negative situation or argument with her man, the decision to punish her man by withdrawing sexual privileges and contact will result in an opposite effect to that which she originally desired to achieve. Remember that we are dealing with a child in this case. Based on this idea, think about how a child would react to being refused an expected ice cream after an argument or negative situation. The only thing that you will achieve from him by denial is this thought: "She doesn't love me.   She doesn't give me any ice cream."   I EMPHASIZE: **"SHE DOES NOT LOVE ME"**.

Let me ask you at this point a small question. That is: "What is the connection between ice cream(sex) and an argument? What are you really going to achieve if you are not going to give him the ice cream(sex)?"

Many women are going to tell me at this point: "How can I even think about sex if I am so angry at him?" The answer offered is that **sex** is the best Italian ice cream in the whole world for your man (sorry, child). To take away sex from your man is the same as taking away ice cream from the poor little child who has been waiting to eat it the whole day long.

So, what is the child to do who has had his ice cream taken away? Is he supposed to sit on the corner of the street and cry, or to take initiative and go by himself to the nearest ice cream shop and find his treat there? There are many shops out there in which to obtain ice cream in various flavors and consistencies.   Do you see the logic that the child will find his way to an ice cream elsewhere? Can you see the logic within the child's soul in this case?

It is the nature of the child to search for pleasure, for love and warmth, and for positive excitement.   Children resent punishment, which is seen as a lack of love. **They do not see what you see**. It would be very foolish of you to punish your man by withdrawing sex once he has tasted it without taking the risk that he will search for it in other places.

Women who punish their men with the sex tool are putting a large risk upon themselves.   There is great awareness today of the many STD's, including AIDS, rampant in society.   Basically, punishment will not educate your man. You cannot educate children through punishment.   Among children, a very strong punishment creates fear on the one hand, and, on the other hand, creates a strong desire to run away from the person who is the source of the punishment. This is also the reason why so many teenagers are running away from home.

However, with the man-child, unlike the child-child, the imposition of punishment will not create fear. What will be created is a huge anger, disappointment, and desire for revenge. **I EMPHASIZE: DESIRE FOR REVENGE**.
These three reactions are a direct result of the man's ego. But, like the child-child, the man-child's desire to run away from home will begin to grow inside him with ever increasing intensity and, at the same time, he will have many

thoughts about finding other women.

The keys are in your hand -- the keys for failure or for success. Most men in our society do not need much to be happy. For the average man, the woman's desire to share her bed with him is the strongest indication of how much **she really wants him**.

Although it is known that both **desire and energy** are needed for **good sex**, your man will appreciate you very much if you suggest that you still make love even though you may be tired and not able to express the usual energy. You must always try to save the connection between you and your man -- **the love connection**.

It is a realization that many women will now say: "I am not a sex machine and ready to have sex all the time. He must understand me too." I agree that this is not an easy task, but it is one that can become easier for you. Sometimes, a nice refreshing shower before you go to bed can awaken a sleepy cat.

****

CHAPTER FOUR: LOVE, GIVE AND TAKE

The soul of a man with a good conscience is like the soul of a child. This child will go with eyes closed to those who will hug him, care for him, and love him. Do not let your man-child run away from you as a result of aggressive words on your part. In most cases, verbal abuse is far worse than physical abuse. A child's soul can be severely injured by humiliation. Constant humiliation will engrave itself on his heart so deeply that it will remain there eternally.

You have no idea of the extent of the damage you may inflict upon your man when you abuse him verbally. For you, a small remark can sound very simple and meaningless, but for him it is a **direct blow to his soul.** He does not hear the exact words that are loudly spoken or yelled out. His childish primitive reaction is: **"She doesn't love me."**

Surely many women will proclaim that it is the man who initiated the verbal abuse -- the screaming, the name-calling, the accusations, etc. Should this be your reaction, it is imperative that you keep in mind the origins of this behavior.

Returning to the starting point, realize that you are dealing with the **soul of a child.** Because the situation evolves around the soul of a child, it must be realized that a child will never be angry at his "parents" unless he has good reason to be, based on his view of course. A child can also forgive quickly compared to an adult, if his soul is touched with love. He will forgive you immediately and accept you as though nothing had happened before.

Most women do not know how to forgive. They carry with them a hidden, unreleased anger for an extended period of time, adversely affecting their man. This anger does not create anything of a positive nature. It will destroy you, people that are connected to you, and your environment. It is like a boomerang. Throw your anger out to another and it will return directly to you stronger. You must learn to disconnect yourself from this anger. You must be able to control yourself to a point that, within a few seconds, you will remove this anger and frustration from your person and concentrate fully on your mission to control your man in a positive way.

We live in a world of giving and taking. Intimate relationships are also built upon this revolving concept of giving and taking. The more ice cream you give to your child-man, the more he is going to do for you. And, I hope that you still remember what the meaning of "ice-cream" is.

For example, let us take the expression of love. Usually, the child is not the first one to say "I love you" to the parent. It is the parent who first, by example, shows the expression of love and verbalizes it with "I love you". Women need to hear these words frequently to feel loved and to feel that they are thought of in a loving manner. On the one hand, it is seen that the verbal expression of love makes women feel loved.

On the other hand, the physical expression of love makes a man feel loved as exemplified by sensual touch and massage of the buttocks, for example.   Most men do not feel comfortable with verbalizing their feelings of love, but show these feelings in other ways.

One way in which a man might show his love would be by taking the initiative to take out the garbage cans.   You might see this as a chore that the man should be expected to do on a normal, daily basis.   However, this is not something that the man enjoys doing.   Knowing this, most women, who see this as a man's job, tend to nag the man until he does it.

However, when the man performs this duty without any prodding, he is performing an act of love,and, unfortunately, it is usually not seen as such.   Rather,   it is taken for granted.

So it is for some reason that men find it difficult to say "I love you", unlike women.   And women have needs much like that of a cat, desiring to be petted and spoiled constantly.   In order to receive the man's attention, his petting and spoiling of you, you must give him **your special ice cream.**

And, once in a while, you should give him this special ice cream adorned with surprises(or toppings) such as chocolate fudge, whipped cream, jimmies, nuts and fruits.

Your man will appreciate this so much, that he will do anything that you will ask him to do.

Let me remind you that all these actions represent a **POSITIVE CONTROL** by the woman.

It is important to remember throughout your reading of this book that most men appreciate, first of all, your sexuality, then, after that, the rest of your qualities.

MOST MEN NEED ONLY THREE THINGS IN ORDER TO BE HAPPY:

SEX

FOOD

SLEEP

CHAPTER FIVE: HINTS

Do not ever forget that when we speak of man here, we are speaking of the soul of a child. A child cannot understand hints. However, the problem is that the world of women is loaded with hints. Sometimes these hints derive from a sense of modesty, sometimes from another source.

Nevertheless, in most cases it is observed that the more intelligent the woman, the more hints she utilizes. Amongst a group of women engaged in conversation, hints are utilized frequently, with all participants understanding the meaning behind them. And, amongst these groups, the higher the average IQ, the greater the number of hints observed.

Herein lies the problem in conversation between you and your man. The "hint language" is very difficult for your man to understand. The child understands only direct talk or direct actions. Therefore, when you speak to him, he will interpret your words exactly as spoken, and, when you act, he will interpret your actions exactly as they appear.

There is a great example here, revolving around the issue of the woman punishing the man through lack of sex. Basically, this punishment is used as a strong hint by the woman to show her man that his behavior, involving an argument or other event that occurred between them, was not appropriate or not good enough. In this case, the man cannot understand the hint.   He can only understand that this punishment came about for one reason: She does not love me or care about me, and that is why she punishes me. **I EMPHASIZE: SHE DOES NOT LOVE ME.   THAT IS WHY SHE PUNISHES ME.**

Man can be very sophisticated in the world of business and in the commerce between men.   But, when it comes to the relationship between man and woman, man is not sophisticated and cannot get down to the root of things. That is why you should never try to achieve anything based upon hints.   **Always be direct, to the point.**

****

CHAPTER SIX: EX STORIES

In the last chapter, it was mentioned that hints are not good. But, sometimes, in relationships, based on his nature, you must use smart tactics or white lies in order to control your man. Most men do not like to be in competition with other men when it comes to a woman. They like to be the winners without a fight, and they like to be the one for you. Let me give you an example:

Let us say that your man is not taking out the garbage cans on time, and it is very smelly around the cans. You feel really upset and tired from the whole situation, and you think he should be taking them out on time without your reminding him to do so. You then decide to approach him in a way that so many women do, a way that is a great mistake. A woman that does not understand the soul of a man will approach him in this way.

So, you approach him in this manner: "Honey, you know that I do not want to sound like your mother, but, before I met you I used to have a boyfriend that I lived with for a few years, who would take the garbage cans out on time like a Swiss watch. I was so happy with this. He gave me great pleasure. I pray and I hope that one day you will do the same. You will take out the garbage cans on time without my asking you to, and I will be happy like I was then."

The damage that is done with this approach is very great. Your man will develop negative thoughts all because you mention your previous boyfriend and how good he was to you. You hurt his primitive ego, an ego that exists in his subconscious from ancient times. This is the ego of a man and a child mixed together.

A child will be hurt when he sees his mother paying attention to children other than him. This is the child's ego. Because you mention your ex-boyfriend in a loving manner, the man's ego part will be hurt because he sees your boyfriend in the present tense as someone you still care for and miss. He sees that you miss the kindness of this boyfriend and the good things that he used to do for you. This makes your man feel as though he cannot match up to your ex-boyfriend. All this talking that maybe he will improve himself and someday match up to this ex only serves to increase his rebelliousness and aggressiveness towards you.

It must be stated clearly that a woman who approaches her man in this way will only produce the opposite effect that she intends to achieve. You must understand something very simple, and that is that you were a "virgin" when you met your man, even though you and your man both know that this is not the case. The less you mention your "ex's", the better it will be for your relationship. **I EMPHASIZE: THE LESS YOU MENTION YOUR "EX'S", THE BETTER.**

Many men will claim that they are not jealous of a woman's past. And women are taking this seriously. With their interest in sharing their past, from time to time they bring stories and photographs of their previous men to show to their current man. On the surface your man may appear calm, as though he does not care, but underneath he is spewing lava like a volcanic mountain. He does not like it at all. He actually hates it.

Every remark that you make about your former lovers brings to your man's mind the lovemaking that used to take place between you and them. I know that this sounds strange, but this is the way that it is. Your man is developing within his imagination a script that is not bringing positive energy to the relationship. A smart woman who wants to control her man in a positive way will **never relate stories of her past men and how well they have treated her.**

Now that I have related, with examples concerning "ex's", approaches to your man that produce negative results, let us return to the example of the garbage cans as previously related in this chapter. The smart woman who wants to produce positive results will approach her man in this way: "Honey, when I was a small child, it was my job to take out the garbage cans. One day, while performing my job, a large rat jumped out of a garbage can and scared the hell out of me. Ever since, I have dreadful nightmares every time I see a garbage can. I know that for you it is difficult to remember to take them out on the appointed collection days, but, if you do, I promise you one thing. Before you go to sleep on that day, I will give you such a great all-over body massage that you will be in heaven. This is a promise that I will stand behind as long as we are together."

What do you think will happen when you relate this to him? Well, let me tell you. Your man will take out the garbage cans every night, even twice a night, not just on Wednesday and Friday. There is one word of caution here. Never ever make the mistake that so many women do who make a promise, but do not stand behind it.

Have you ever been in a situation where you promised something to a child but did not stand behind the promise? Do you remember what happened? There was a strong impact on the child's soul. Research shows that the damage incurred in this situation will remain with the child for the rest of his life, creating low self-esteem and lack of trust.

Your man will react in exactly the same way, except that he will not show it to you. He will try to take revenge against you later on. You promised him your sexuality as a reward for his action. You must understand that for him, your sexuality/love(or whatever you choose to call it) is the most important thing in his mind. **When you do not stand behind your promises, he sees this as a deception and disrespect for him.**

He is taking this very seriously, so seriously that you cannot have a clue to the depth of the seriousness. To you it may look like a bad joke, but the damage you have done is very severe. Do not ever promise your sexuality if you cannot stand behind it. Never promise him anything you cannot stand behind. Do not destroy him. Build him slowly, ever so slowly, and in a wise way, so that he will be under your control, and he will do anything you want him to do with desire, anticipation, and fondness.

Many women will tell me: "I am not a sex machine who is ready to go all the time. I have my problems too, and he must understand this." But, as I reiterate repeatedly, if you have any doubts that you will stand behind your promise, then do not promise. You should not promise the best ice cream if you cannot give it to him. But do give him a reward you can promise to give him, and do stand behind it. If a full body massage is too much for you, then promise him a back massage, for example.

Again, you must understand that **this ice cream is the most important thing you can offer him,** even though he may appreciate your beauty, intelligence, friendship, social standing, etc. So, to make it clear, good sex between you and your man is on the top of the pyramid in his eyes.

VIRGINITY

Before, the concept of virginity was mentioned as related to your man's perception of you. Many women will say: "How can he think that I am a virgin in his mind? I wasn't a nun. I did not spend my life in a nunnery. We live in the 20th century. Society is very open and things are different than before."

The point is that the man knows in his subconscious mind that you are not a virgin, but he likes to think that you are.

Although your claims are very true and down to earth, we have here a conflict between the way that your man thinks and the way that you think.

But you have forgotten something. Your man has the jealous or envious soul of a child, combined with the primitive male ego of ancient times. Therefore, if you put these two things together, you will see that it is not worth relying on modern statements that are a reflection of the sophisticated, intelligent brain possessed by woman. Your man is not at all sophisticated in this case.

Your man, having the soul of a child, interprets events in much the same way. Children love fascinating stories. When they hear such a story they remove themselves from reality and become a player in the story. This explains why your man, when he hears stories about your "ex's", feels that the story is real, that it is happening now. Even though he may not have met your "ex(s)", in his child's imagination he can see in front of him your former lover's(lovers') naked body(s) next to yours, and this is killing him. Far worse is the situation where your man has met your "ex(s)", and it is so much easier for him to see the two of you together in detail.

Many men cheat on their wives for various reasons. The average man will not cheat on his wife without a good reason for it in his eyes. I am not saying here that most of the cheating is the fault of the woman. Rather, much of the cheating belongs to problems that are attached to the man such as lack of maturity, lack of understanding a serious relationship, etc.

However, the average man who does cheat does so because of mistakes made by the woman in the relationship, mistakes that have come from her desire to control the man in the negative way rather than the positive way. It must be repeated continuously throughout the course of this book that the man needs to be controlled with a wise, positive control -- not a clumsy, negative control.

The man-child is building in his mind throughout the years tidbits of information that he is being fed by the woman. This information may derive from past stories that have been related to him and from the woman's opinion on many issues. So, basically, the line between imagination and reality does not exist in many cases in the man-child's mind.

Having exposure to this knowledge, you must be very careful with what type of information you supply to your man. The best advice I can give to you is: **Do not mention your past sexual experiences.** Do not tell stories about your ex's(s). Do not tell stories about your past relationships with other men. Even if he asks you for this information, do not give it to him. In his subconscious mind, he does not really want to hear about it. Lightly pass over the subject and feed him positive energy by telling him how good he is. Tell him that you do not remember much from the past, a past that was negligible compared to your experiences with him now.

✳✳✳✳✳✳✳✳✳✳✳✳✳✳

CHAPTER SEVEN: RED LIGHTS

RED LIGHTS is a fundamental, strong and important chapter in this book. So much aggravation could be saved if you were to see the red light when it is shining at high beam. Before going into details on this subject, be reminded that not all men can be placed under the same category. The type of man covered by this book is the normal, sensitive man who still retains conscience.

Such men as these are qualified to come under positive control. Of course, there are thousands upon thousands of men out there who do not fit this criteria. This specific group of men are called the **red light warning men.**

In the first moment that you meet a man that fits into this group, he will set off a warning sign which we shall call the "red light" from now on. Unfortunately, most women ignore this red light. Then, deep into a complicated relationship of which they wish to separate themselves from, they find themselves dealing with much pain, loss of time, loss of money, deep frustration and, often, loss of good health.

THE FIRST FIVE MINUTES OF TRUTH**

Now, to go into details, the first consideration should be **THE FIRST FIVE MINUTES OF TRUTH**. The five senses can show us only 1% of what is actually going on around us. But, those five senses are sufficient enough to warn us of a dangerous situation and to be aware of the appearance of the **red light**.

Usually, the **first five minutes** are the most **critical** moments to check out the man upon meeting him for the first time. In those few moments, your senses are very sharp and very alert, and you can see details in a very clear and sensitive way.

After those first five minutes, this awareness will **dissipate**. The first impression in those five minutes is usually the **right impression.** In those moments you are still not affected by the man's power or energy. You are in complete control, because you **want to be in control**. You check out every move of the man and every word that he speaks. You are simply in control. Your brain is receiving accurate information and reflecting this in your state of mind. You have a very sharp picture.

You can see the red light if there is a red light, and you can see the positive energy if it is there. Basically, you see everything.

Suddenly, a very unique and dangerous situation occurs. The man begins to speak to you. He is **taking control** and you are losing it. In your subconscious mind you know that you are starting to lose control. You no longer see details or messages that your brain imparted to you so clearly just

moments before. In this moment, you have lost control.
You are entering the world of illusion, a world that appears
so promising and so nice, but yet it is still an illusionary
world. It is not true, it is fake. In your subconscious mind,
you paint the red light a nice green color -- a color that says
the danger is over; there is nothing to fear. Green means
go.

Now you are deep in a whirlpool of illusion. It sucks you
in, and you have no desire to fight it. Everything looks well
and fine. The dangerous situation is over. You enjoy every
moment.

Why did you paint this red light in a green color? Why do
so many women in our society do this? Why, in a clear
mind, do they go into a disastrous relationship creating a
disaster that can last years and cause so much damage upon
going out of it?

If you only knew how to stop in those few moments of
truth, you could save yourself a lifetime of pain and
suffering. Why, after awakening from the first illusion and
seeing all of the red lights shining and the warning bells
ringing do so many women still ignore these signs and
demonstrate no desire or power to change?

The following example will demonstrate the meaning of
ignoring the red light through an analogous situation.
Imagine that you are driving all alone through the Arizona
desert. You have been told that the road is very dangerous

and that you must reach your destination before darkness. It is a very hot day when, suddenly, a warning light appears on your dashboard which indicates that there must be a leak in the cooling system. At this time, you remove from your console a container of paint that you keep there for such emergencies. And you paint over the warning light on your dashboard. In a split second, the warning light disappears and you are happy again.

Would you like me to continue this story? Do you catch the point? Does this sound silly? Do you see the similarity between this case and what we mentioned before? I am sure that you see it.

The explanation for this situation comes from several sources lying within the woman herself. These are:

1. LOW SELF-ESTEEM

2. FEAR

3. A SMALL AMOUNT OF MASOCHISM

Most women who do not stop at the red light are usually suffering from low self-esteem or lack of confidence. This situation usually is rooted in childhood and displays itself strongly following the demise of a bad relationship.

Basically, when a woman in this situation sees the red light, instead of running away, **she refuses to see and ignores the problem.** Or, perhaps, she is mentally tired and too weak to fight. She puts herself in illusion, the brain's protective device.

Many women will probably say now: "How can I recognize the red light?" The simple answer is: The moment you see the red light you recognize it, but, you are afraid of it. You must stop immediately and say to yourself: "I must do something. I saw a red light. I must not ignore it. I must stop and change direction. I shouldn't let fear control me. Fear can paralyze. Fear can create illusion. I must be in control all the way."

When an emergency situation occurs, your senses or instincts tell you immediately. They refuse to let you go. They do not let your brain rest. Your brain is bombarded by red lights that are telling it constantly: "Stop! Stop! Emergency!". Clarifying and summarizing this process, it may be stated that a red light is a warning sign of your mental immune system. THIS SYSTEM IS GIVING YOU THREE MESSAGES: "DANGER. STOP. RUN AWAY."

Your mental immune system is not aware that you suffer from low self-esteem, and that you have decided not to fight anymore, but to put yourself in illusion, giving up on any ideas that you deserve the very best. You simply decided that you do not deserve the goodies, and that another woman deserves them, because she is better than you.

Many women that refuse to stop themselves in a moment of emergency are letting the fear control them, as has been mentioned before. They live in a state of partial masochism, meaning that they believe that they do not deserve happiness and satisfaction. And that is why they do not stop themselves in these critical moments (red lights).

They push themselves purposely, without any logical explanation, into dead-end relationships with men. They know that the man they are with is not the right one, but they push themselves into a state of illusion, thinking that the **man will change** and everything will be okay. The deeper they are in this bad relationship, the greater the illusion. They then reach a point wherein they accept the situation as it is and totally give up the fight. Here is where that frightening expression of partial masochism displays itself in the attitude of such women. Now, they know for sure that they do not deserve happiness and that they will never ever find the right man.

Let us stop here for a moment, and describe further the concept that the **man will change,** and the woman's desire to change the man.

The most common mistake that women make is the attempt to makeover their man, i.e., to change his nature from head to foot. Their goal in doing this is seen as a step in the professed control of their man. Unfortunately, **people do not change.** However, in their hopes of utilizing a means to an end, they may appear to change. They may behave in a different manner in a particular situation, depending upon what they wish to achieve in the situation. But, again, there is no general change in human nature.

The positive control method is not designed to change the man's nature. The positive control will create a situation in which the man will behave the way the woman desires him to, but only if this behavior is worth it to him. If it is not worth it to him, he will never let it happen. I EMPHASIZE: HE WILL NOT LET IT HAPPEN IF IT IS NOT WORTH IT TO HIM.

A smart woman will wrap her man around her small finger with a lovely smile, a sensual touch, a hot kiss, and sensitive words when making love.   This, along with all the other strategies and sensual approaches that only women know of and practice, will create a positive control.   Your man will love it, he will demand it, and you will be in the clouds.

Now, to return to that concept of partial masochism and the situation resulting from those women who have given up the fight, we can observe its long lasting effects on the libido of women.   Although aware of what is going on, these women still stick to a very low level man, a man that will humiliate them and control them with a strong hand.

So, the moment a woman anticipates a bad relationship, such as this, she is immediately losing the most important thing she can own -- self-esteem and self-confidence.   The moment that she loses these valuable things, she has lost everything.

The best advice for women experiencing mental weakness, low self-esteem, or any other negative state is: Do not enter into a relationship. When you are aware of these states of mind, **beware**. You must take time out, even if it will take many months to recuperate. You must become stronger. You must be able to reach the point that **when you see the red light, you will have the power to stop, to say no, and to say that: "I will not continue even one more step in the direction of this trap. I am in complete control. I will not let any man control me. I deserve happiness. I deserve satisfaction. I deserve pleasure. No other woman is better than me. I am not afraid of anything. Nothing will influence me. I control the fear. I am in complete control. I will choose the right man, at the right time, when it is comfortable for me. No one will pressure me on this issue. I am not a game, and no one will play with me. I am in complete control."**

And then, little by little, you will find yourself with a high self-esteem, and you will reach **the top of the pyramid. Let us now talk about the pyramid -- what it is, and what it means.**

THE PYRAMID LAW

Our world basically operates by the pyramid law. You can see that just about any issue comes under this law.

Let us say that on the top of the pyramid is the 1% , and the rest of the pyramid is 99%. Let the 99% represent 99 people, and the 1% represent 1 person. (Please see illustration on page 33.) Following are a few illustrations utilizing this law:

Illustration number one: In a group of 100 people, only 1 is a millionaire, and he is on the top of the pyramid, which is the 1%.

Illustration number two: If we take a group of 100 women, only 1 woman in this group is really gorgeous, so she belongs on the top of the pyramid, which is the 1%; the others belong in the rest of the pyramid, or the 99%.

Illustration number three: If we take a group of 100 men, only 1 man is your man. He is the one who will make you happy for the rest of your life, and he is on the top of the pyramid - the 1%. The rest of the men are in the 99% part of the pyramid, and are the **99 red light men.**

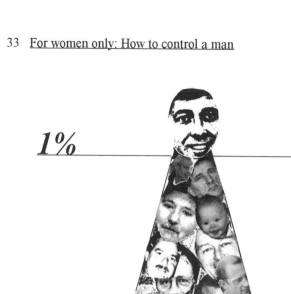

1%

99%

Your goal is to reach this unique individual who will match you 100%, and who does not bring up any red lights. He is the perfect man for you, and your mission is to find him. You must listen very carefully to the pyramid law. **This knowledge will change your life forever.**

There are only two ways available to find this man. The first is the **difficult and long way, which is ignoring red lights. The second is the easy and short way, which is a complete stop at red lights with a change of direction.**

I EMPHASIZE: A COMPLETE STOP AT RED LIGHTS WITH A CHANGE OF DIRECTION.

Now you are ready to go. You are ready to meet the man of your life. This is the man that is at the top of the pyramid, the man with qualities of warmth, sensitivity, conscience, loyalty, trust, passion, understanding, respect, patience, etc. This is the man with all the qualities that you know **you deserve without compromise**.

You are now taking your own future in your own hands, without any pressure and fear. You are in complete control. You are on the way.

You will meet those 100 men on different occasions. You must find the hidden one. To remind you again, you have two ways to find him. You can choose the difficult and long way, or the easy and short way. Let us start with an illustration of the difficult and long way.

Going out on a first date with a man from the 99% group, you see a red light in the first five minutes of conversation. You decide to continue the conversation and to ignore the red light. And so, you give him another chance on a second date. The second date becomes a third, and a fourth, and so on. You see many red lights, but you like to paint them green because you have chosen the difficult way. Now, you are in a serious relationship. Many years pass by with ups and downs, and thousands of red lights that you paint green.

Suddenly, you sober up. There is no more illusion. This is a time of awakening. You feel the urge to change the situation, to run away. It is tough and it is painful. Many years have passed by and many people are involved. Perhaps there are children, pets, and finances involved that result in a complicated situation.

You have decided to go out of the relationship, and you exit. You find yourself desperate. You need love, and you need warmth **now and only now. You need immediate gratification.**

Your mental defense system is so completely weakened and out of balance that you are completely in chaos. And then, history repeats itself in your moment of desperation.

Instead of waiting and taking time out to rebuild your self-esteem, you take the fast solution now. And, again, when you meet another man from the 99% group and see the first red light, you immediately ignore it because you do not want to see it. You want love and happiness now, and you do not want to wait. The whole situation repeats itself, just like an old movie viewed repeatedly.

Again, many years pass by. Time is running out, and you are not young anymore. The chance to now find this one man at the top of the pyramid is close to zero.

Basically,   studies have shown that if a woman is choosing the difficult way, it will take her from two to three years minimally to burn out in a relationship with the wrong man.

Let us assume that there are 99 men to experience on the route to finding the 1 man at the top of the pyramid. And let us assume that the bad relationship with the red light man is taking an average of two years. If we take 99 and multiply this figure by 2, we have a total of 198 years. So, in order to find the right man following the difficult way, you need to live in this world a total of **over 200 years.**

To take an example that is not so difficult as the one above, let us assume that you find the 1% man after experiencing only 30 men. At an average of two years for each red light relationship, we then have a total of 60 years before you find the right man the difficult way. And, assuming that you began this search at the young age of 20 years old, you would then be 80 years of age before finding the right man. Do you think that the solution is to take many strong vitamins, minerals, and tonics to be in decent shape when you meet the right man at the age of 80, or to choose the short way? What makes more sense to you?

Therefore, you can see that a woman must choose the short way to find the man in the 1% category. Now, just what is the short way?

Let us return to the explanation of the pyramid law. I have stated that there are 100 men, and your man is hidden between them. Now, you have the first date with a man from the 99% group. However, now **your decision is to do what you should do when you see a red light.** You go to dinner with the man and suddenly feel uncomfortable with him. There are many things about his behavior that are bothering you, that touch a nerve. He is not polite enough, he makes a lot of noise in the process of eating, he seats himself at the table before you are seated, he opens the driver's side of the car before opening the door on your side (the passenger side), and any other example that affects you personally. **Some women see certain behaviors as a red light while others do not.**

At this point, let us stop for a moment to give further explanation on the meaning of the red light. A red light is a personal thing that a woman sees as negative in a man's behavior. Certain behaviors are seen as a red light for some women, whereas other women would not see them as such. Every women has her own set of expectations and values. That is why red lights reflect a very personal point of view. **Again, every woman knows deep inside what for her is a red light and what is not.**

When you experience a red light, realize that this red light is only the tip of the iceberg. In other words, what behavior brings on the red light is only a hint of the intensity to come. So, it is easy to say that if you multiply this initial behavior by ten, this will be the man's behavior later in the relationship.

For example, if you go out to dinner with a man, and the man is making some noises while he eats, and you see this as a red light, you can then expect that these noises will be ten times as loud further into the relationship. The claim that many women and men have that they cannot see a red light is totally unacceptable, because it is no different than the claim that they cannot see the difference between good and bad. A normal person can choose between good and bad. It is only an abnormal person that cannot make that distinction. The normal person can differentiate between a dangerous situation and one which is not dangerous.

Now, to return to you and your dinner date. You are sitting there at the dining table and, having already seen a few red lights, you become uncomfortable. This time you have decided to take control and to stop at the red light. When you stop, you truly stop. You do not continue on past the light. You think and consider the situation. In this moment, your brain is working in a concentrated matter and everything is very clear, because you did not put pressure on yourself. You have come to a very positive and definite conclusion. The conclusion is that the red light is real and you do not want to continue even one more step in this relationship. So, in a very polite way, you tell the man to go to hell.

The woman who knows how to stop at red lights is at a very high level of consciousness. She will never accept a prototype, and she will always go for the original and authentic model.

Returning to the pyramid law and the length of time necessary to find the right man(1%), let us examine this time in view of the short and easy approach. Assume that it will take an average of 3 days for the wise woman to decide if she will continue the relationship with the man from the 99% group. Figuring that all of these 99 men will bring up a red light for this woman in the first five minutes of conversation, and multiplying this figure of 99 by 3, we arrive at a time of 297 days(approximately 10 months) before she can find the man of her dreams.

Now, to return to the second example that we cited with the short approach, let us assume that this woman finds the 1%

man after experiencing only 30 men. At an average of three days for each red light man, we then have a total of only 90 days(approximately 3 months) before the **right man** can be found the short way. So, no matter which example is taken here, it can be seen that the right man will be found in a period of less than a year, if a woman is taking control and utilizing the short and easy approach.

On the other hand, if a woman is ignoring the red lights and choosing the long and difficult way, it will take her a lifetime and more to find the right man.   So, remember, when you see a red light, stop and change direction. **I EMPHASIZE: WHEN YOU SEE A RED LIGHT, STOP AND CHANGE DIRECTION.**

****

CHAPTER EIGHT:
MAN'S BEST FRIEND

A man's penis is one of the most important things in his life. A man sees his penis as his most important and best friend. Most men give their best friends a nickname. The name given his best friend is based upon his desires, dreams, personal tastes, or ambitions. For example, many men with a small penis give their member the name of "Goliath", "Jumbo", or "Gorilla". On the other hand, men with a huge penis have adopted names for their friend such as "Little Boy", "Shorty", or "Pee Wee", for example. The name given all depends upon the man's point of view and the way that he views his life.

There are many men who give a name to their penis based upon their occupation. For example, men in the army may assign such names as "Tank", "Cannon", "Can Opener", "Rocket", or "Machine Gun" to their member. Many police officers may call their penis "Door Knocker", "Expandable Baton", or "Responder", etc. Construction workers like such names as "Drill", "Hammer", or "Steel Rod", etc. Names such as "Hose", "Fire Extinguisher", or "Lifeline" are popular with firefighters. Lawyers may prefer names such as "Shark", "The Judge", or "Terminator". Some names that physicians may assign to their penis are "Knife", "Probe", "The Healer", "Needle", "Scope", etc.

A wise woman will accept the name of her man's best friend in a positive way, and will use it each time that the sex object is arising. Your man will appreciate it more than anything. This idea sounds very strange and stupid, but you have no idea how important it is in the eyes of a man. The moment that you show passion or love to his little friend and mention his 'holy' name, you break many barriers along the way to controlling your man.

Many men sometimes change the name of their little friend throughout their lifetimes, depending upon what they are going through in life. For example, a man who called his little friend "Moses", and then had a best friend by the name of "Moses" die, will then change the name of his best friend. I had a friend who by the age of forty had already changed the name of his member twelve times, and he is still not finished with his assignments.

The age at which most men begin to call their penis by a name is usually twenty on up. It is probably because, at this point, the man has developed a greater awareness of the little friend hanging in such a proud way between his legs. A wise woman, noting the importance of this friend, will address her man's little friend as a third member of the relationship and give him his due reward, knowing this to be an important step in the positive control of her man.

A woman can utilize this approach in either a serious or humorous manner. We can take the example of going to a swimming pool where the water is really cold, but both you and your man jump in to savor the fun. After the first shock of hitting the water, you could then address your man in this way: "I hope that "Jumbo" will not catch pneumonia because I really like him and would love to have him visit me in the evening. Please keep him in good shape." Another example would be the time of lovemaking. Between moans you should mention the little friend in this way: "Give me "Jumbo. I missed him so much," etc. Your man will be in the clouds. He will think of what you told him for the next twelve hours until you see him again.

THE SHAPE OF MAN'S BEST FRIEND

Many women have often wondered if there is any way that they can determine, in advance of actually knowing, the size and the shape of a man's penis. There have been many theories on this issue, but these are only theories and not concrete proofs. Of course, the best way to know is to see and experience the man's best friend. But, we then know that it is too late.

Now, let us go to the most common theory abounding this subject. Basically, the shape of the fingers can relate to the shape of the penis. However, the most accurate finger to observe is the forefinger(or index finger) and not the middle finger as most people think. This middle finger is only used by the man for warm-up exercises.

Going into depth in the study of the index finger, let us observe its particular thickness. The base of that finger represents the base of the penis, and the nail or tip area of the finger elongated in its direction represents the head of the penis and its general direction in erection. For example, if the finger is wide and short, please use your imagination. And if the finger is long and narrow, use your imagination again to form a picture.

Another theory concerning the size of the penis revolves around the size of the foot. This theory is less accurate than the first one, but can give a fairly good indication of the size of the man's best friend in most situations. Another plus to the first theory is its practicality. When seated at the dinner table, it is a lot less obvious to stare at a man's hand than his foot under the table.

Now that you are educated, you can determine the relative importance of this information in your relationships. But do remember that this is still just a theory and, in many cases, may be far away from reality. The tried and true method is direct experience.

Nevertheless, there are some women who are aware of the fact that the true sexual power of a man is not measured by the size or girth of his penis. It is measured by the muscular structure of his lower back, buttocks, and thighs. These are the three most important areas in supplying the strength necessary to perform well. So, the **technique** is always more important than the appearance.

A smart woman who is interested in a strong male to provide strong sexual activity will check very carefully the structure of his lower back, the shape of his buttocks and thighs, and then, after that, the structural build of his little friend. Some say that 6" is a good erect length to waken up the thousands of nerve endings in the woman's vagina, which is considered the average length of a man's penis in that state.

THE SIZE OF MAN'S BEST FRIEND AND THE EGO BEHIND IT

Men give a lot of respect to those men who carry between their legs an instrument of large proportion. For some reason, both men and women think that a large penis is an expression of the sexual power and potency of its owner. It is also expected that a large penis will bring greater sexual satisfaction than one of normal size.

Looking to facilities where large congregations of men work or are incarcerated(e.g. army bases, jails, military schools, etc.), the sight of an exceptionally large member rising above all the others creates a very strong respect for the gentleman in possession of this wonderful sight.

I remember that when I was 20 years old and serving in the army, there was a soldier in our group of average build, but carrying a huge penis between his legs. The moment we beheld this sight in the public shower, the group of soldiers started to give him a great deal of respect and admiration. This man could not believe what had happened to him. He could not understand why he was given so much respect. When he was not around, we could not stop talking about his penis. We used to tell dirty jokes about it, but we all knew, deep, deep inside, that we were all disappointed that we were not the personal owners of this great tool. Sometimes, we even felt jealousy.

Basically, it does not matter if the average male out there possesses a high IQ, a strong position in society, or a respectful job, when it comes to the male sexual ego the male behaves like an animal all the way. Many men, when going to a public restroom, will take a glance at the person nearest them to see in that split second if their penis is large or small or may represent a threat. This animal behavior is so deep in the subconscious mind, that most men cannot even see or feel that it is happening to them. (Remember that this applies to **many men, not all men.**)

Another place where this behavior is widely demonstrated is in the health club or gym. There, in the locker and shower facility, a man who is well endowed will strut like a peacock in front of the other men, knowing the ego power that he possesses above all the others.

Again, most men in their subconscious minds, think that the lucky man with a large penis is so strong and can supply so much pleasure to a woman, that he is invaluable in the eyes of women. This phenomena is prevalent in the mind of almost every man. Almost every man dreams of having a larger penis, concerned that his own member is not large enough or good enough. That is why many men prefer underwear that is designed to enhance the size of their penis, maybe in the same way that many women prefer brassieres that enhance the size of their breasts. In some cases, both sexes even resort to surgery to fulfill this dream.

At many Halloween costume parties, you can often see that many of the male guests will come dressed with a long coat which, upon opening, reveals a humongous, snake size, well hung penis. When other men view this apparition at the party, they do not view it with the humor that women do. The reason for this is that they really feel deep inside that they should have a larger penis than they possess, and viewing another guest wearing such a costume only serves as a slap in the face reminder.

Relating these facts to the methods of positive control and understanding the mind of the man when it comes to his penis, **it is evident that a smart woman who really wants to control her man will remind him at every opportunity that she is really pleased by the size, hardness, and power of his penis**.

By reciting those positive features of his little friend, she will create a situation wherein the man will demonstrate even more power, perhaps hidden power, than he had ever demonstrated before. He will satisfy her on a higher level than before. A smart woman must tell her man that she has never before seen such a large, beautiful, and powerful penis and demonstrate her adoration of it by continually touching and stroking it.

Let us stop here for a moment, and demonstrate a negative example related to the power of man. This example is completely the opposite of the nature of this book, because this book is based upon a positive method of control.

A woman who seeks to destroy her man in a few seconds will tell him: "Honey, I do not know what happened to you. Your penis is shrinking, and is not the same as I once knew it. It is weak. It is soft. In my opinion, you should go to the doctor to have it examined." If the woman continues to speak this way over a number of days, she can create in the man a condition of impotency that can affect him for the rest of his life. This example is extremely destructive, and should not be utilized until all other means to escape a red light relationship on its final legs have been exhausted.

BLOW JOBS

In the eyes of a man, the blow job is not considered to be the ultimate sexual pleasure. Many men also cannot reach orgasm by way of the blow job. However, it is extremely important from other aspects.

Although women in general do not take readily to administering a blow job unless they feel particularly intimate, warm and loving with a man, men feel a very high ego gratification when receiving this type of attention. A man feels that the woman, if she goes so far, must really love or care for him. On an emotional level, he feels as though he is on the stairway to heaven.

There are many women who do not want to hear about, discuss, or think about this idea. They feel that giving oral sex to the man is disgusting. But, a man who is not receiving oral sex from his woman will first try to convince her to perform this act. Then, after failure to do so, he will try to find this pleasure elsewhere. It is not because he needs other women, but because he feels that there is something missing in the relationship. He takes the situation personally to heart. He cannot understand that she feels she cannot do it because she is disgusted - that this is not the only reason, as he cannot be sure that it is just the oral sex that she is disgusted with. Maybe, he feels, it is another problem with him that makes her feel that way. Even if she says: "Honey, it is not you. It is the idea.", he still thinks: "She doesn't care enough. Why are other women doing it?"

So, basically, a woman who wants to stay in a committed relationship and one devoted to monogamy, must get used to the idea of giving her man oral sex and demonstrating her pleasure in doing so.

****

CHAPTER NINE:
FIDDLER ON THE ROOF

In the muscial and movie titled "Fiddler on the Roof", a married couple in a small Russian village had only daughters and no sons. During the period of time in which the play takes place, it is a shame not to have a son. This concept reflects a phenomena which still occurs in many countries in the world today.

What is this phenomena? In many countries in the world, most especially those in the third world, the macho man is at his peak when his first son is born. He will receive great respect and a strengthening of ego from his male peers and family. Such a man is automatically considered a very potent and virile man, and there is no doubt about his capabilities in the bedroom. In such a society, this man has very high self esteem, and is very happy with his life. (In many modern countries, many men still carry this idea in the subconscious mind.)

On the other hand, a man who only fathers female children suffers from very low self esteem because it is apparent to all who know him that he must be weak and powerless in his performance in the bedroom. This man will do anything in his power to bring a male child into the world. His wife may have to suffer through many pregnancies until a male child is conceived. Sometimes, you can see in such societies, families of fifteen daughters and one son who is the youngest child. In such cases, the father has finally , in his old age, redeemed himself. He will leave this world with a smile on his face. However, if he should fail throughout his life to bring a male child into the world, his wife will bear the brunt of the blame and he will be miserable for the rest of his life, as will his wife.

There are modern ideas which revolve around the concept that the desire of men to have a male child is rooted within man's desire to produce an offspring that will look, act, feel, and behave as he does. This idea rings true for a small representation of the men in modern society. **But the true reason that the majority desire a male child is to appear as a strong male in the arena of sexual performance.** As such a male, no one may contest his talent and capabilities. The more male children that a man has, the more respect he can demand from male society.

I have experienced this phenomena myself. Many of my male friends used to laugh at me because I have three daughters and think that, maybe, underneath all my muscles and shows of strength, that I really lack potency. These types of remarks came from men that I would never expect to hear such things from - people that you would expect to be less primitive.

Nevertheless, everytime that I was at a barbecue, picnic, or pool party and the subject came to children and families after the meal was consumed, most of the men conversed in such a way that I thought I was with a bunch of Mongolian warriors gathered around the campfire measuring and comparing the size of their penises. I reached a point that I felt very uncomfortable during these gatherings, and I did not know how to change the conversation. Whenever I tried to bring logical explanations into the social discourse, the other men would put me down and tell me that I was only making excuses for the real problem.

However, I could not allow this situation to continue. Since I have a good imagination and look to solve problems whenever they occur, I could not wait for the next pool party. It did not take long for me to find myself in the same situation. But this time, when the men started on my problem again, I told them that I had a very serious confession to make. Suddenly, everybody was quiet. I insisted that the women at this party draw closer so that they might also listen to my confession.

I took my time and made a very dramatic presentation to this group of twenty. My confession started by my relating that I must face reality and deal with the problem that I had. I went on to explain my past difficulties in explaining "my problem" and the decision I had reached to solve the problem that day once and for all.

First of all, I requested that all the women at the party tell me when they would have a day available, and I wrote these dates along with their names on a large sheet of cardboard. They all gave me different days, in which I arranged a period of two to three hours for each one. After the details were arranged, I then asked their husbands to sign on a sheet of paper that stated: "I am an open-minded person. I will let my wife participate in a three hour experiment." After all the men signed, and silence reigned again, I told them that my plan is to share my bed with each of their wives for three hours each, after which time they could tell their husbands if there was any connection between having daughters and the ability to perform well in the bedroom.

The reaction was similar to that of the explosion of an atomic bomb. The men were totally silent, while the women were joking and laughing. I won this round with flying colors, and from this moment on I earned my dignity and respect from my friends. No one brought this issue up again.

The real truth about this issue is that there is absolutely no connection between the performance of a man and the end results in the delivery room. It is well known that among pilots and other male employees who work frequently in the skies, that the percentage of female born children is far higher than that of male born children. During the time the above story took place, I used to work for a large airline and I was in the air many hours nearly every day.

So what is the connection between this story and a woman in control of her man? A smart woman with far-reaching vision and modern ideas should be very careful to check the origins of the man she is with before embarking into a serious relationship. If her man came from a country where the macho beliefs that were stated before exist, and a strong relationship is entered into, this woman will suffer inexorably later on if her man is unable to produce a male child.

She will find herself placed under extreme pressure from her husband to reproduce until a male child is born.   She has two options: (1) either to accept the pressure and multiple pregnancies, which may not be favorable to her, or (2) to refuse to participate and then to find herself rejected by her husband and thereafter replaced by another woman.   In any case, she will lose.   If she has chosen to participate, and after repeated attempts has not produced a male infant, she will receive the blame from both her husband and his family. They will point at her as the source of this inadequacy.   It is a losing situation all the way.

I EMPHASIZE: CAREFULLY CHECK THE CULTURAL ORIGINS OF A MAN AND THEIR INFLUENCES ON HIM BEFORE EMBARKING INTO A SERIOUS RELATIONSHIP.

****

CHAPTER TEN:
THE FOUR GROUPS OF MEN

Most men have an inclination towards women of a particular body type. There are four such groups, as follows:

Group A: Weakness towards large breasts
(approximately 40% of men)
Let's call them the "Breast men".

Group B: Weakness towards a full, shapely bottom
(approximately 35% of men)
Let's call them the "Butt men".

Group C: Weakness towards shapely, well-formed legs(approximately 20% of men)
Let's call them the "Leg men".

Group D: Weakness towards a beautiful face
(approximately 5% of men)
Let's call them the "Face men".

Each of these groups displays a different sensitivity to a woman's body, seen most strongly upon first introduction and early dating.   This sensitivity still exists later in the relationship, but is not displayed with such openness and expression.

Some men favor more than one part of a woman's body, but still retain their preference for a particular part.   For example, one may find men that belong to Groups A & B consecutively(breast men and butt men), but they will still be drawn more strongly to one part over the other.   The best test for a man like that is to pose a question to him: "If something were to occur in nature that left women with only one of these four parts(breast, butt, legs, or face), which one would you most like to see?   This question refers only to sight, not to touch.   So, which part would you most like to see?"

It is important that you recognize and acknowledge this weakness and determine which group your man fits into before going into a relationship.   **In order to control a man, the smart woman files this information in her brain and utilizes it to her best advantage**.

Here are some examples that illustrate this situation.   First, a man from Group B(The Butt Men) for some reason starts a relationship with a woman possessing large breasts and a diminutive behind.   In the future, this man will find himself becoming dissatisfied in the relationship, longing for the large bottom that he does not have. Second, a man from Group A(The Breast Men) will find himself frustrated later in the relationship if, for some reason, his woman's breasts have decreased substantially in size, depriving him of his "special pleasure". Another example is a man from Group C(The Leg Men), who later in the relationship with his woman, sees that she has gained weight and lost the shapeliness and tone of her legs, imparting to them much thickness and flabbiness along with the appearance of being permanently rooted to the ground. This man will be suffering interminably.

In many cases, as in the examples just given, the man being deprived of his preferential part will begin to take action to satisfy himself. At first, he may purchase pornographic movies or magazines that display the parts that he is sensitive to. Later on, he may visit Strip Clubs or Nude Bars and, in a few severe cases, he may look for another woman who will satisfy his preferential craving.

Mario, a manager of a large computer firm in Silicon Valley, California, was 30 years of age and ready for marriage. He was tired of all the games and longed for a serious relationship and a family of his own.

One day, he was eating his lunch in the company dining room when he suddenly felt his eyes drawn towards a beautiful secretary on her lunch hour. He felt something that he had never felt before. She was almost perfect in his eyes, a beautiful woman with long shapely legs, a cute and strong, small behind, and very comely breasts.

Mario could not control himself, so he went over to her table and began to strike up a conversation. Her name, he discovered, was Susan. Into the conversation, he found her to be a bright and witty woman with a winning disposition and smile. She liked him immediately, drawn to his dark and sensual appearance and his easy conversation. Also, she was attracted to his background of Italian descent and the promise of hot blood.

With these fires burning, things began to happen very fast. Eight months into the relationship, Mario and Susan decided to get married. After a short time, Susan became pregnant, and nine months later they were the proud parents of a baby girl. Both Mario and Susan were very happy. Everything seemed perfect.

Their arrangement was such that Susan stayed at home with the infant girl while Mario continued his employment at the computer firm. One morning, Mario's car would not start. The battery was dead. Susan suggested that he take her car and, since she was going to be at home anyway, that she would be more than happy to call a mechanic to replace the battery in his car.

Mario was already late and jumped on this offer like a person in quick-sand handed a rope. After Mario left, Susan called a mechanic who came and fixed the problem with Mario's car. While the mechanic was busying himself under the hood, he asked Susan to turn the ignition of the car on and off. At this time, Susan took note of the great mess inside her husband's car. She had not seen the interior of his car for sometime, as they were accustomed to using her car when going out, with the convenience of the infant seat already installed there.

After the mechanic left, Susan decided to do her husband a favor and surprise him by cleaning his automobile interior. To her surprise, she discovered hundreds of pornographic magazines. She was in total shock. Gazing at a few of the magazines out of natural curiousity, she found that they all had something in common. Displayed freely were the shapely bottoms of women, many in sexual doggy-style positions.

Going back into the house, she found herself very confused. For her, this was a new discovery. She never realized that her husband was so deeply involved with these magazines, and many thoughts came into her mind. She decided to go back into the car and search even further, although she felt uncomfortable doing so.

However, she knew that she must find out what was going on. In the glove compartment she found many brochures from Strip Clubs and Nude Shows in Las Vegas. On many of the brochures, an address was marked by a circle around it, indicating that someone had some interest in this specific address and phone number. Now she was even further in shock. Mario used to go to many conventions in Las Vegas for his job.

In the next few hours she was in complete chaos. Many thoughts came to her mind. At seven o'clock that evening, Mario returned home. Susan did not wait long. She asked him to sit down for a serious discussion. Mario was nervous. Susan mentioned the mechanic's visit and her assisting him by turning the ignition on and off, and then stated her surprise at discovering all the pornographic magazines inside his car. She told Mario that she really wanted to know what was going on.

At first, Mario tried to explain that the magazines were the property of his best friend who had asked him to keep them for him. But Susan knew him too many years. He could not lie to her. In a moment of truth, Mario told Susan of a hidden desire he had held inside dealing with this material. Every time that he visited Las Vegas, he had to go to see naked women, especially women with fully sculptured, rounded behinds. And he had no explanation of why this was the case.

Susan was concerned that he went even farther, but she did not ask him about it. She suggested that he go to a hypnotherapist to see exactly what the problem is. She also insisted on being involved in this process all the way, being constantly informed and made a part of the solution.

After many appointments with the hypnotherapist Mario found, the results came out. In his subconscious mind, Mario was unhappy with his wife for only one reason. Mario, from a young age, showed a strong sensitivity towards the buttocks of women. From early on, he constantly gazed at such buttocks and commenced dating women possessing behinds of an attractive and shapely proportion.

Before he met his wife, all the women that he dated shared in common a fully rounded and shapely behind. Mario never thought about this and never realized that this sensitivity was so strong in his mind. He was a typical Group B man(The Butt Men). Mario loved his wife deeply and was happy with his marriage. Everything was **almost** perfect. Mario's subconscious desire was never fulfilled, as Susan did not possess the type of buttocks that he so desired.

If Susan had been aware that almost every man had a weakness for a particular part of a woman's anatomy, she would have investigated immediately as to Mario's particular preference upon meeting him. Nevertheless, Mario should have been aware of his specific weakness and should have taken it in a serious manner.

Unfortunately, everything was far too involved and complicated by the time they both made these discoveries. Moreover, Mario loved his wife so much, and they were such a perfect couple, that he went to the best psychotherapist out there, who gave him direction as to how to live with his frustration. The therapist suggested that once in a while, before having sex with his wife Susan, Mario should watch a pornographic movie having his preferential features of a woman's body in full view on the screen, and to place these visions in his mind while making love to his wife. Pornographic magazines could also provide the same visions. The therapist warned Mario not to discuss this resolution with Susan, since the actuality of the problem would only serve to make Susan feel inadequate and dissatisfied during their lovemaking. Susan never knew of this solution and everything returned to normal.

In this case, the solution was close to perfect but still not perfect for Mario. **The best solution is to be aware of this phenomena and to take the proper steps having the knowledge in hand.**

THE EXPLANATION FOR THE "WEAKNESS PHENOMENA"**

Every woman has a sex symbol on her person as explained previously by the "four groups" of male preference. For example, if a woman with large, full breasts appears by surprise onstage in front of a group of 100 men, she will find that she has excited 40 of these men. In comparison to her, if a woman with a full and shapely behind will appear under the same circumstances, she will find that she has excited 35 of these men. This percentage reaction will occur in likewise fashion should a woman with beautiful legs or face appear on the same stage. This example is cited to clarify the sensitivity to particular parts of the woman's body as perceived by men.

There are several theories for this phenomenon. One theory looks to the man's childhood as the source of his particular attraction. When the male child first becomes sexually alert, he will become attached to the part of the woman's body he first perceives in its naked state. This will affect him with increasing strength as the years go on.

For example, if a child saw his beautiful teacher exposing a pair of beautiful legs in a miniskirt in his math class, he would from that time on be sensitive to a woman's legs. Or, another child that observed his female neighbor through a window making love in the female superior position, and viewing her from the rear, would then develop a sensitivity to the buttocks of women. As mentioned before, there are some men who have a sensitivity to several parts of the female anatomy. In light of this theory, such men may have as a child viewed a woman totally naked These men may claim sensitivity to more than one part, but there is still always one part of the female anatomy that they favor over another.

Before we continue with the second theory which pertains to animal instincts, let us understand more about the connection between these instincts and lovemaking behavior.

In the middle of lovemaking there are many men who sound out loud noises similar to that of a horny lion or bear. **Usually, the men making these type of noises are considered very hot compared to the men who are quiet during lovemaking.** Also, these loud, expressive men feel much freer during their lovemaking than do other men, which brings the sexual relationship to a very high level. They tend to perform better because of this feeling and are considered to be better lovers.

Conversely, **a man who is troubled and unable to release his stress and frustration even during lovemaking, will be unable to perform with intensity and satisfaction.** This is a well known fact.

So basically, a man who carries with him many problems in his mind will transfer these problems to the bedroom and never achieve a high level of performance. We can also say that if this man will continue these negative thoughts throughout each day and night, he may reach the point where he has become impotent.

In conclusion, the man who makes loud noises in the bedroom while making love is in a stage of complete release from any negative thoughts and in an expression of the total animal instincts alive in him. A woman who feels, in the middle of lovemaking, that her man is too quiet may change the situation by whispering in her man's ear: "Honey, I want to hear you growling like a horny bear. It turns me on. Please do it." By doing so, she will not only assist in releasing negative thoughts in her man's mind, but will serve to gain for herself far greater satisfaction. **A man who is completely released of negative thoughts can bring a woman to a level of orgasm that she has never experienced before.**

As we have mentioned before, **the key is in the woman's hands.** She can decide if her life with her man will be a life of beauty and satisfaction, or one of boredom and frustration. A woman can train her man to behave in a particular way in all aspects of the relationship - sex, friendship, partnership, family life, etc. **Contrary to common belief, the man is actually interested in being trained in this manner, since he will benefit from it. A woman can achieve anything that she wants to by following the messages received from this book.**

The power is in your hands to change your life. You have a mighty power in your feminine sexuality - a power that only a few women know how to utilize. It is pure foolishness to accept the axiom that men are more powerful than women. A woman thinking in this manner has not achieved the higher level of consciousness that leads to the use of positive control through **feminine sexuality.**

The second theory relates to the level of animal sexual instinct in the mind of the man. This level varies from man to man. For example, the 35% of men who are sensitive to the buttocks of a woman derive their sensitivity from the animal instinct. In nature, the male animal is attracted to the rear of the female animal, as they like to approach from the rear. The male animal is constantly sniffing, licking, and caressing the rear of the female in anticipation of close gratification. This explains why this 35% group(Group B: The Butt Men), prefers to make love doggy style.

Group A(The Breast Men) is considered less animalistic than Group B(The Butt Men). They prefer lovemaking when the woman is in the superior position astride them, so that they can observe the movement of the breasts back and forth, up and down. When a woman is with a Group B man and prefers the superior position, she can train her man to enjoy this position as long as she allows him the pleasure of the rear approach as he nears orgasm.

The Group C(The Leg Men) men prefer making love face to face, but preferably with the woman's legs folded upwards and caressing the man so that they may be viewed and touched as much as possible during the course of lovemaking. It is also important that the woman have her partner suck her toes as part of the warming up exercises or prelude to lovemaking. When doing so, the woman must be careful to protect the image of exclusivity in this area.   In other words, if asked, she must not reveal that she has experienced this prelude of toe sucking with another man, but relate this as an idea developed exclusively for her man's pleasure.

Now, when it comes to controlling the Group D(The Face Men) men, the woman must pay constant attention to the neck and face of the man, suggestively licking these areas as part of the warming up exercises, for example.   During lovemaking, she should also lick, lightly bite, and caress these areas.

Emphatically, I must stress that the weakness a man has towards the particular part of a woman's body prevails throughout the day, in all areas of life.   It is not just specific to the act of lovemaking.   Therefore, **a smart woman will utilize this knowledge by allowing her man to constantly observe and to touch the area that he is sensitive to.**

For example, a woman with a man from Group B(The Butt Men) will accentuate her buttocks with tight, revealing clothing in that area so that her man may continually take notice.   And, every now and then, to draw attention to the connection, she will lightly brush and caress the penis of her man.   At the same time, she should request that he massage her "sore buttocks" to allow him the pleasure of that touch he so sorely needs.

Referring to the example of the breast man(Group A) in this light, a smart woman will utilize clothing that reveals and uplifts her breasts so that her man may constantly take notice. She will go to him and suggest that he suck her nipples to alleviate congestion, and allow him to caress and kiss her exposed breasts from time to time. And, as in the example of the buttocks man, she will suggest the connection by lightly caressing the penis of her man.

All of these ideas represented here are for the purpose of maintaining sexual tension.

****

CHAPTER ELEVEN:
SEXUAL TENSION

What is sexual tension? **It is a state of continual positive tension, maintained at a constant level.**

Basically, if a man is not under this tension, he is not under control. Conversely, the greater the level of tension, the more the man is under control.

A strong sexual tension can last even after lovemaking. Of course it is going to be less powerful, but will still exist at a level based upon the woman's approach. To keep a man in sexual tension is an art that not every woman is capable of fulfilling, whether through lack of knowledge, lack of will, or lack of experience. It is not easy to acknowledge or think of this issue in daily life.

However, at this point, there are two questions that a woman should address to herself. Should she work hard to maintain a constant level of sexual tension which will lead to her full control over the man and, later, to a happy relationship? Or, should she make the choice not to keep the man in sexual tension with the end result of chaos and a problematic relationship?

In this case, the old saying that to keep a relationship stable and happy requires a lot of work and energy is very true. The reaction of many women at this point will probably be the realization that it is their role to activate the relationship and to keep the man happy. They will complain that no one is given the responsibility for making them happy.

Remember that your man is like a child. A child does not realize your need for attention. A child is selfish and blind to the needs of others. He has not reached the level of understanding that your needs are just as important as his.

Your job is to control this child, to train him, and to bring him to a level wherein he will behave differently than his basic nature. You can do it. You have the power to do it. And, you have all the tools in this book to enable you to do it.

Man was born to be lead by woman through positive control by means of sexual tension. He must be kept in sexual tension all the time. This will keep him in a constant state of expectation. He will look forward to receiving your "goodies" in the right amount at the right time.

Following are a few examples illustrating methods of keeping a man in sexual tension in day to day life. First, viewing a scenario involving the leg man(Group C) and his wife, a nurse, during a weekly work day, we can see the workings of this tension. The wife, before going to work, will inform her husband that she expects her legs to be very sore after a 12 hour shift on her feet. She requests playfully that, upon her return home, he should give her legs a thorough massage with warm sesame oil, while at the same time gently caressing his penis. This man will maintain a state of tension and anticipation all the day as he works, anxious to get home and await the arrival of his wife.

A woman in a relationship with a butt man(Group B) and tending to work in her home garden during the weekend, will wear tight shorts as she works and continually maintain positions wherein her buttocks are projecting out or up into the air. As she calls out to her man to assist her by bringing tools or materials she needs from time to time, she will ensure that he is able to view these positions as she works. And when he comes to her side, she will gently caress his penis and buttocks while allowing him to touch her strategically exposed bottom. This man will not be able to wait until the gardening is completed.

The breast man(Group A) is leaving for work in the morning two hours before his wife must leave. She remains in her loosely wrapped robe during breakfast, carefully ensuring that her breasts are partially exposed. She bends over to kiss her man as he eats, fully exposing her breasts to his face as she does so, and encouraging him to caress them with his lips. Simultaneously, she gently brushes his lap, lightly touching his penis and scrotum as she does so. She then sits directly across from him at the breakfast table with her breasts partially exposed to his direct view. This man will think of her breasts all day long and anticipate his return home from work.

It is a work day and the face man(Group D) is eating a bagel with cream cheese and drinking coffee before heading to work. His wife is sharing breakfast with him as she readies herself for work, and is beautifully groomed. As he finishes his bagel, she notices some crumbs and remnants of cream cheese on his face. Before he has a chance to wipe these off with a napkin, she licks the crumbs and cream cheese off his face while gently caressing his penis. Then she gives him a kiss and a caress on his neck. He will be in heaven all day long.

However, the best method of maintaining sexual tension on a day to day basis is to make love in the morning prior to work or other activities.

Making love in the morning creates many positive benefits for both parties simultaneously. In the first place, a concentration of endorphins occurs. Scientifically speaking, these are peptides produced by the brain that react with the brain's opiate centers to create a feeling of pleasure.

Secondly, both the man and woman will benefit from the more relaxed and positive approach they will have in starting out the day. Often, in modern society, we tend to arise in the morning with a negative energy, thinking of all the demands we need to face and the tasks we have to accomplish over the day, immediately putting ourselves in a state of tension and uneasiness. This is the worst preparation we can give our bodies to begin the day. The act of lovemaking will reverse this mood, relax us, and start us off with a calm and focused mind, all the better to face the tasks ahead.

Thirdly, and most importantly in relation to this book, is the sexual tension that will be strongly maintained through the practice of sex in the morning. It is like giving a jump start to a car with a weak battery. The engine will immediately warm up and maintain its charge throughout the day. **The man who receives sex in the morning is under a very high sexual tension control throughout the day. A smart woman will send her man out of the house in the morning fully satiated. He will not have cravings for his ice cream.**

Another suggestion to enhance this method of creating sexual tension is to create an environment in the bedroom that will fulfill the need of man to have visual stimulation. This could be, for example, the addition of strategically placed mirrors throughout the room, on the walls and possibly even on the ceiling. Men are very strongly affected by visual stimulation, compared to women. They must see what they are experiencing and do not rely so much on the imagination.

Therefore, providing this visual stimulation to your man will enhance sexual tension by giving him a visual memory to carry him through the whole day. You will control him remotely, and he will think about you continuously, awaiting the next morning with anticipation.

Many men and women choose traditionally to make love in the evening. Unfortunately, the effect of the endorphins at this time is not the same. When going to sleep after sex at night, the conscious effect of these endorphins is wasted. You may feel wonderful immediately after the love-making, but then you fall asleep. In contrast, endorphins created with morning love-making will last from one to two hours, and the memory of all those pleasurable feelings will last throughout the day.

Should a man and woman having sex once a day be in the habit of making love only in the evening, it is highly suggested that they change their behavior to making love in the morning. If it is at all possible, it is highly recommended to make love two times a day, both morning and evening. This will provide an even stronger connection between you and your man and an even superior method of maintaining sexual tension. Your man will feel good all day and sleep well all night.

Many men arise in the morning with an erection. This may be due to the cyclical phenomenon of recurring erections every 90 to 120 minutes throughout the night, with one appearing upon arising, as well as the influence of the higher levels of testosterone appearing in the A.M. So, it may be concluded that nature has already made them receptive to sex in the morning.

In many foreign countries, a large number of women are already following the ideas in this book, including the concept of sexual tension in general, and, particularly, **sex in the morning**. Because of this, a type of joke or saying is heard often in these countries, which basically states: "I like to make love in the morning." Foreigners visiting these countries who ask to learn a phrase in the language of the country are often learning this sentence first, and by saying it to the natives gain a positive acceptance with much hearty laughter.

No matter what, it is always helpful to be creative in your approach to keeping the man in sexual tension. Sexual tension may be likened to the continual warming of the kettle after it has reached the boiling point, wherein a constant hot temperature is maintained so that the tea or coffee may be prepared again at any time.

Keep the home fires burning and the kettle constantly on the stove.

****

CHAPTER TWELVE: TERRITORY

Man is a territorial creature. The establishment of territory is a natural part of his behavior. Most men are not aware of this behavior in themselves, and claim that this behavior does not exist in modern man.

Man's behavior varies drastically from a crowded area to a secluded one. A woman who feels she is not receiving enough hugs should take her man to a crowded city or crowded beach. There, subconsciously, he will feel the urge to hold her close and to protect her. This is the territorial urge.

The source of this behavior lies within the nature of primitive or ancient man, from a time when man's personal space was his protection from all outside threats to his survival and well-being. In his subconscious mind, he feels threatened by the other males around him in a crowd, and is ready to fight in order to protect his female.

But, if a woman should go with her man to an isolated area, she will immediately see a different behavior. Her man will feel free of worry about any threats. He may distance himself more, feeling no need to protect. However, if another man should appear on this scene, he will suddenly become protective again. He will think: "She is mine and no other man may gain claim to her."

There is a subconscious body language that exists among men regarding their territory. The average man can immediately sense who, among the men around him, is threatening, and who is not. The other men in the area can also feel if your man is capable of protecting you or not.

Sometimes you may find men who have the nerve to approach you while you are with your man. They feel that he is a weak man, and not strong enough to protect you. When other men have this feeling, they will immediately pursue the woman and flirt with her accordingly. This action is the modern rendition of an ancient ritual wherein the stronger man would fight the weaker one and run off with his woman. **Subconsciously, this is the instinctive reaction to the urge to mate.**

Most women will enjoy this type of flirting in certain situations. But, this game is a little bit dangerous. If the man is of a sensitive nature and does not react to the situation, he will retain the memory of this experience inside of him, and it will constantly dig into him like an embedded knife. In the future, such a man will try to regain his lost dignity. If the woman should continue to accept such flirtations and repeat this behavior in the future, such a man may turn into a woman hater whose only desire is to achieve revenge against women.

Basically, men are hurt more than anything by attacks on their manhood such as humiliation and taking of their territory. In a woman's eyes, this behavior appears to be very primitive and childish, but this is the way that it is. It is very difficult to change this behavior.

As we have mentioned before, your man is carrying feelings that are deeply rooted within his subconscious mind from ancient times - feelings towards territory, feelings of fear, feelings of threats, jealousy and revenge.

For example, John and Julie are a young married couple who enjoy going out dining and dancing for an evening together. They are married four years, having married young at the age of 22. Julie is an extremely attractive and sexy woman with an outgoing personality, who seems to draw people to her no matter where she goes. She accelerates this attention by smiling and flirting with those who are drawn to her, and she glows in the light of the attention she receives. This is something that she somehow needs. She gains great enjoyment in particular from the attentions of strange men.

Many times when John and Julie are out dancing together, Julie is invited to dance by other men and she acquiesces. Sometimes the dance is very hot and sensual, sometimes very slow and close. Many of these men, enamored of Julie, send drinks or flowers to her table in appreciation of her charms. It almost looks as though John is nonexistent.

However, Julie is really crazy about John and the relationship has been very good. They are good friends as well as lovers. John is an attractive man of slight build and very fine features. Some might say that he is almost effeminate in appearance. He has a calm and soft voice, and a laid-back nature. One might say that aggression is not his strong point. He dresses smartly and is well-groomed, making a nice appearance but not one that stops the show.

In the beginning of the marriage John very much enjoyed their evenings of dining and dancing together. But, shortly after this, Julie began her practice of flirting and accepting dancing invitations from other men. At first, she had feelings of guilt that she might be hurting John and would ask him how he felt about her dancing with other men. John did not reveal how he really felt deep inside and indicated that he really did not mind. However, the seeds of negativity began to grow in his belly, although he did not express this outwardly. He would seethe with jealousy and anger as he observed her increasing closeness with other men.

There was a deep-seated reason as to why John could not say anything to his wife about his real feelings. Seeing his wife as his best friend, he felt as though she should be sensitive to his feelings and aware of what he was really thinking. For him to tell her not to behave in this manner would be to put his dignity down. It was a "Catch-22".

Julie did not understand what she was doing to John, and John did not want to say anything because of his male ego.

After a few years, the situation worsened. John found himself surrounded by strange thoughts of revenge. Suddenly, he felt hate towards his wife. All the pictures of evenings out in the past came to his mind, pictures of men holding his wife close and kissing her on the cheek, sending flowers and drinks to the table, and showering her with attention. He could not stand it anymore.

Every Friday, Julie would go to visit her parents in a nearby city. On the 17th of August, a Friday, Julie left her home early in the morning for her usual visit. She would normally stay for five or six hours at her parents' home, but on this particular day she was not feeling so well. Upon awakening that morning, she felt as though she were coming down with a cold and was not particularly ecstatic about making the trip. Nevertheless, she decided that she would not let her parents down.

John did not work on Fridays, but preferred to stay at home and accomplish what tasks were needed around the house, as well as catching up on his paperwork. He would wait for Julie's return from her visit, after which they would go out for dining and dancing together.

Upon arriving at her parents' home this particular day, Julie already felt hot with fever. Her mother suggested that Julie make this a short visit and return home early to nurse her cold. After two and one half hours, Julie was ready to leave. Her mother suggested that she give John a call from their home to let him know that she would be arriving home early. But Julie told her mother that she preferred to call him from the cellular phone in her car when she would be about forty-five minutes drive from her home.

After thirty minutes of driving, Julie decided to call John. To her surprise, there was no answer. After fifteen minutes she tried again, but still no answer. She was really concerned since John customarily carried his wireless phone around the house or yard and there was no need for him to go shopping since they had already done so. After twenty-five more minutes she arrived home to find a red Jaguar parked next to her husband's car. Julie had never seen this car before and did not know to whom it belonged.

Before stepping out of her car, Julie decided to call her husband again. There was no answer. She started to feel uncomfortable and had feelings of surprise intermingled with feelings of worry and anxiety. Following her instincts, she decided to enter the house from the back door by the pool area, which could not be reached until unlocking the gated door of the pool area's heavy wood fence. She walked by the fence surrounding the pool until she reached the back door.

Placing the key in the lock, Julie heard the sound of giggling and a splash of water. She froze in her tracks. Instinctively, she attempted to observe and interpret the sounds coming from within the pool area. Suddenly, she heard her husband's voice saying: "Honey, do you want something to drink, or shall we do it now?" There was an answer immediately from a female saying: "Let's just do it now!"

Julie could not believe what she was hearing. She decided to open the gated door a crack and to take a look at what was going on in the pool. However, remembering the loud creaking noise the door would make once the key was turned and it was opened, she thought of another strategy.

The irony of the situation was that she had so often complained to John about the noise and had asked him to oil the door hinges, and to take care of the large space beneath the door whose easy access to animals and other unwanted creatures had bothered her. Now, in this case, his not having made the repair to the door was to her benefit. She took out a small cosmetic mirror from her handbag and placed it underneath this door at the right angle to view the swimming pool area. As she did this her hands were shaking, but she soon steadied herself enough to make the proper placement.

Gazing into the mirror, she was shocked beyond belief. She saw John's naked body lying on the inflatable mattress they used for romantic evenings in the pool. Above him was a young, beautiful, naked woman performing oral sex. Julie was disgusted and full of anger. She could no longer keep the mirror placed in a stable position. Tears of anger and sorrow began to choke her. She ran away as fast as her legs would move her back to her car and drove like crazy for two hours, not knowing where she was going or what she was doing.

After this crazed journey, she returned home and discovered that the red car was no longer there. Julie entered her house with red and swollen eyes covered with globs of spread eye makeup from endless crying. John, in the kitchen, yelled out to Julie upon hearing her enter: "Julie, I was worried about you. I called your parents' home to see when you had left. They thought that you had already arrived home." Julie, entering the kitchen, met John's eyes and screamed out at him: "You pig!"

Later in the evening, following the fireworks, John confessed to his wife that it had been more than a year that he had been cavorting with call girls at their home every Friday that Julie visited her parents. He also confessed that the main reason for his actions was based on revenge because of her behavior every time they would go out dining and dancing. Her continued flirtations with strange men over the years had constantly ground into his manhood. After so many years of feeling his dignity swept from under his feet, he confessed that he now felt nothing but hatred for her.

Four years after these confessions, John died of complications from AIDS in a small apartment he had rented following the divorce from his wife. Eight months following John's demise, Julie died of complications from AIDS in her parents' home, surrounded by family and friends, a few of which were former dance partners. The smell of the flowers these men brought to her deathbed was the same as that of flowers she had received during her marriage to John.

****

CHAPTER THIRTEEN:
SELF-DEGRADATION

In the chapter on "Red Lights" there is a lot of information regarding self-control prior to entering a serious relationship. In contrast to this, I will explain a situational behavior involving lack of self-respect that is practiced by many women seeking a relationship with a successful and powerful man. The end result of this behavior is lack of control by the woman, humiliating treatment by the man, domination by the man, and loss of dignity for the woman.

In order to understand this unique behavior, let us go back in time several hundred years and try to understand what went on in the conscious and subconscious mind of the women of that era.

Back then, the position of the male was very clear. His job was to provide food, shelter, and clothing for his wife and family. The male was a good provider and very strong physically. Physical endurance was a good indicator of success, since most good positions in society required strength of body.

Today we are facing a very rapid development in technology and jobs resulting from it. This increasingly rapid rate is far ahead of evolutionary development. The subconscious mind of the woman has not kept up with the changes brought about by this technology, and it is still influenced by this past way of life.

If we go back just a few years, as technology began its rapid and steady climb, we can find that those individuals possessing a high IQ and flexible mind became those considered successful in our society. Now that a few more years have passed by, we have observed and experienced a revolution in roles within the family and workplace. In today's modern society, most **women can support themselves without the assistance of men and, accordingly, without the accompanying dependence on men.**

In spite of these facts, the idea that a woman must find a successful and powerful man still exists in the woman's subconscious mind. This desire is very strong in most women who equate the meaning of "being rich" with being powerful and successful. The modern translation of these attributes, in other words, is money. It is difficult for most women to hide this desire, and most men are aware of it.

Hundreds of libraries could be filled with thousands of volumes containing stories of the women who fell into traps created by men aware of this weakness. A man whose wallet is not thick enough will find many ways to impress a woman with stories of his success, wealth, and connections, so that the woman will view him in a positive manner. By so doing, he can then achieve his end goal of putting her in bed as quickly as possible.

Returning for a moment to the Red Light chapter, we may view this woman as perceiving a red light during her first conversation with a man. However, her desire and hope to establish a relationship is so strong that she paints this red light green.

When I was twenty-five years old and working in Europe, I had experiences that may well illustrate this point. While travelling with empty pockets, my desire was strong to entrap a female as fast as I could. Back in that time, I used to work in a special capacity for a large airline. Along with a few co-workers of similar intention, we often spent long periods in luxurious hotels as part of our position, since the airline had special arrangements with these facilities. So, although young and broke, we found ourselves residing in an atmosphere of wealth, luxury, and grandeur.

To save money we had many tricks that we utilized in the hotel in which we were staying. For example, if a breakfast tray were placed outside another room, we would collect it and ravage the meal ourselves. To enjoy coffee at a minimal cost, we would heat water with an electric coil and add instant coffee.

A hotel in Amsterdam in which we stayed had a nightclub belonging to the hotel on the lower floor. Many desperate women seeking rich men came to this nightclub, aware that the affluent guests of this hotel also enjoyed using this particular nightclub. Our goal was to entrap some of these women.

We knew that we needed a good, sensible story that would explain how such young men were able to be such long-standing guests in the hotel. The story was that we were the sons of rich businessmen on a mission to find new markets, investments, and business connections in this country. Since this could take some time, we were boarded here until our mission was complete. The idea was to find women who would spend some money on us until they discovered the truth. At that point, we would move on to new victims.

We would approach these women who, thrilled with the aspect of wealthy companions, would take us everywhere in their automobiles. They went to bed with us very fast thinking that they were making a good investment. Sometimes, we were discovered quickly. But, as we became more expert in the art of deception, our experiences lasted longer.

A friend and I, on our first attempt, met two women at the bar and invited them up to our room. They did not hesitate to accept our invitation. After entering our room, we inquired as to whether they would like some coffee. Without thinking of what I was doing, I went to the wall receptacle and proceeded to heat up some water with the electric coil sitting on the carpet. The women immediately asked: "What are you doing?" In a very naive way I responded with: "Heating up the coffee". After one and one-half hours, we lost them forever. I made a major mistake that I would never forget, but, as always in life, you learn from your mistakes and improve upon yourself.

Therefore, the next time we invited two women up to our room and offered them some coffee, a plan was in the works. This time, I made a telephone call to a friend in another room who was ready to receive my call and had dressed himself as a waiter. He immediately made some coffee in his room in our usual manner and placed the coffee on a hotel tray along with several croissants remaining from other guests' leftover breakfasts that we had collected in the main hall. He proceeded to add some decorative napkins to the tray along with a bud vase from the lobby, and then headed directly to our room.

When he knocked respectably on the door, I opened it and he placed the tray on the table. I gave him a $100 tip. This $100 was the mutual investment by the group for special occasions such as this. The "waiter" kissed my hand and bowed repeatedly in the Japanese manner, thanking me incessantly. It was difficult for us to contain our laughter, but we did. Glancing at the women, we could see that they were very impressed and we knew that we would have a hot night that night.

This is only one story of the way in which men try to fool women. In many cases, women are fooled by nasty men with a long range plan to fully undermine and destroy their lives. My example from my own life was one involving young men just looking for fun and excitement.

Women who are searching specifically for a wealthy man, often put themselves down in front of such men. They leave themselves open to hurt, humiliation, and ridicule. The moment that such a man has realized that a woman is looking towards his pocket, he will start to behave in a disrespectful manner towards that woman. **Later on, he will fully control her.**

A rich man never knows for sure if a woman is staying with him for the thickness of his wallet or the bulkiness in his pants. Does she truly love him for who he is or for what he represents and can buy? (Here we are not referring to a situation in which the game is fully known to both parties. Sometimes the man is aware of what the woman is after, but is accepting of it, as long as he has complete control of her and she is accepting of this.) Once this wealthy man is in control of the woman, she becomes his toy or trophy. Later on, the recipient woman can go into a depression so severe that no money in the world could draw her out of it.

Women must understand that it is necessary for them to repress these thoughts and desires to catch a rich man. They should acknowledge the arena from which these thoughts and desires are based, and to realize how out of place they are in modern society. Also, they should be aware of the lack of stability of wealth today. Many millionaires arise from the dust, while large corporations go out of business at ever alarming rates. The man who is rich today may be poor tomorrow. Conversely, the man who is poor today may be rich tomorrow. So, **basically we live in a world where the only stability is lack of stability.**

Women of the world, you must understand that you do not need a wealthy man to live in this world in a comfortable manner. You do not need a man with connections to be "in". **You do not need money to be happy.** Happiness comes from deep within yourselves, and not from material things. This is a fact.

The power is within your hands to change your way of life. The men in our society are born to give you satisfaction, pleasure and happiness only after you discover the **secret** of controlling these men in a positive way. The moment that you allow a man to feel that he is the one controlling you, you have lost the whole game.

A man that will feel good, comfortable and happy with his mate and her control over him, will do anything in his power to give her happiness and to improve upon her lifestyle. Money is only important up to a point. The moment that this hidden line in life is crossed, the power of money to maintain happiness is nonexistent. We must discover happiness. It is within all of us.

The moment that we begin to be jealous, to be greedy, and to live in fear, we destroy our integral happiness. Our integral happiness can begin to bloom once we have destroyed these characteristics and face life in a positive manner.

Unfortunately, in our society, we can see many women considered "over the hill" and still possessing an unrealistic list of requirements for the "perfect man", such as: (1) money(equal to power), (2) head full of hair(equal to beauty), (3) muscles(equal to strength and sexuality), (4) connection in society, (5) intelligence, and (6) morality and values.

A woman who is self-actualized and not dependent on men will go for the following list of requirements: (1) a man with a golden heart, possessing morals and values, (2) intelligence, (3) strong communicative abilities, and (4) attractive, if possible, but not necessary.

I remember an ad in a South Florida newspaper placed by a successful doctor looking for a woman with the end view of marriage. The list of qualifications was almost equal to the list required of an astronaut flying to the moon. This doctor was probably aware of the weakness most women have towards power, money and security.

Thousands of women sent their resumes and letters to the Post Office Box mentioned in this ad. It was the largest group of women to collectively put themselves down. What a humiliation! What a shame! Who promised the potential winner - the woman chosen who would become the wife of this successful doctor - that her life would be a bed of roses? Who promised the woman that this doctor would be a "perfect man" and not just a "perfect wallet"? And who promised her that his wallet would be an open book for her?

This is an example of the illusionary state that many women choose to put themselves in. This dangerous illusion will lead to self-destruction, to lack of respect, and to self-humiliation that reaches such a low level that there is no way to reverse the damage.

It is time for such women to think of themselves as an equal in society and to lift their self-respect back up. No man can make a woman happy if she puts herself down in such a manner. The man can be rich, middle class, poor, or whatever. It does not matter. **The happiness will come only if this woman will control the man in a positive way.**

****

CHAPTER FOURTEEN:
LOW SELF-ESTEEM

Low self-esteem is a very important issue. A woman who has low self-esteem may cause herself to suffer for the rest of her life. Most women are not aware that they suffer from low self-esteem. This lack of awareness can last many years until a point is reached where the woman realizes her problem and tries to seek help.

A woman who wants to control her man but suffers from low self-esteem will never reach her goal until she solves her personal problem. Surprisingly, there are many women in our society who have reached a high position(such as doctors, lawyers, etc.) who you would not expect to suffer from low self-esteem, yet in fact they do. Basically, low self-esteem exists at various levels, changing based upon the mood of the individual, the present moment, and at certain points of life. Following are a few examples which illustrate low self-esteem at various levels and degrees.

Linda is seated in an airplane next to an obese but outgoing gentleman. On the one hand, she finds conversation enjoyable with him but, on the other hand, she feels compressed in her seat and lacking oxygen.

After the dinner meal is served, the man falls asleep. Now she feels even more claustrophobic, especially with him leaning on her. She really feels very uncomfortable. Looking around, she sees several empty seats not far from her.

Instead of changing her seat, she remains where she is, thinking for a lengthy time if she should move or not. She thinks to herself that if she should move to another seat and this man should wake up and find her there, he would think badly of her. She does not want to hurt him.

After two hours of flying time, the situation has not changed. The man is still asleep and Linda is completely out of balance. After two more hours, the same situation exists. When the captain informs the passengers that the plane will be landing in ten minutes, Linda is overjoyed.

What happened to Linda in this four hour flight? Linda knew what was good for her and what she was supposed to do, but for some reason she did not do it. **The reason was low self-esteem.** In this case Linda suffered four hours, with maybe an additional four hours to recover.

But what about situations in life that go on for years without any decision to make a change? In such a case, this suffering may not occur just for four hours but, possibly, for a lifetime. All this floundering is happening inside you, **affecting no one else but you. You and only you are affected.**

Let us analyze for a moment this situation involving Linda on the plane. By not moving to another seat would she have really hurt the large man? And even if she did hurt him a little, could this not possibly be a kind way to alert him of his obesity? Maybe it would even lead him to a diet and a healthier lifestyle. Is Linda existing in this world simply to avoid damaging anyone?

Is this her mission in life? By not doing anything is she creating a better society?

In order to invoke change in the society in which we live, we sometimes have to forgo politeness in some ways and to scream and to say: "I don't feel comfortable. I deserve more comfort and more satisfaction. Hey, don't step on my feet." Maybe if Linda complained to the flight attendant or airline company, special accomodation would be given to overly obese people so as not to abuse the rights of more normal people. But Linda decided to be passive. She was afraid to do what she really wanted to do, and the only reason she didn't do it was low self-esteem.

Jenny started working as a secretary for a large long distance telephone company. At lunchtime, many employees would sit in the lounge and relax. This lounge was situated adjacent to the lunchroom.

One day, Jenny was relaxing on the sofa in the lounge with a cup of tea after eating her lunch. Nearby at the coffee machine were two managers who proceeded to question Jenny. "How is the new job?" "How do you feel sitting in front of the computer so many hours?" Jenny replied half-jokingly : "The job is okay, but I have tenseness in my neck and shoulders. I............"

Before she could even complete her response, one of the managers was standing behind her massaging her neck. Jenny was surprised by this action. Everything happened really fast. She barely had acquaintance with this manager, having seen him only a couple times briefly in the last few days. She felt really uncomfortable. Many thoughts came to her mind. The main idea was to tell him to stop immediately. She was very nervous.

The manager continued massaging her neck as though it were the natural thing to do. She felt as though she should stand up and run away. She wanted to push his hand gently away and tell him that she could handle the situation just fine, but she was unable to do this. Jenny sat there frozen.

When she could not stand it anymore and was ready to bolt, the thought came to her that he might be hurt. Maybe this was not really an overt sexual message and truly a friendly gesture. But deep inside, she knew that what he was doing was wrong.

After a few more minutes, the manager ceased the massage and returned to the coffee machine, joining the other manager. The other manager was gazing approvingly and snickering. This was the evidence that Jenny's original thought was correct. Jenny left the room in a hurry. Following this incident, Jenny was afraid to enter the lounge room again, to pass by this manager's office, and to look into his eyes.

After a few days, the phone by her desk rang. The manager was asking her to bring some files to his office.

For several months, the manager repeatedly requested visits to his office with various materials. He would ask Jenny to stay longer in his office just to talk. Massages were offered. He tried to catch her alone many times. Although his behavior was polite, Jenny felt his intentions. To make a long story short, after several months Jenny quit her job and left the company.

In this case, Jenny represents thousands of women suffering from low self-esteem at a certain level. This phenomena initially creates fear, then paralysis, placing the person suffering from it in a situation wherein they are unable to do anything. **They are not in control.**

Let us assume, for a moment, that Jenny has high self-esteem. She feels good about herself. A long time ago she decided that, in every situation, she must be in complete control. What do you think that the "new" Jenny, with high self-esteem, would do if the boss started massaging her neck in this situation?

That Jenny would probably push his hand away in a gentle manner and tell him that she doesn't need any massage. She would relate that if she should need a massage, she might then ask him to do it. **In that moment, she is taking control and totally changing the atmosphere in the room.**

Wherein Jenny, in the second case, decided to stop the process, it was a decision based upon seeing a red light. **To remind you, when you see a red light, you must stop and change direction.** (See Red Light chapter.)

She could also just stand up fast and tell the manager that she had to leave the room for an emergency. This would also work. But, again, the whole idea is to stop the process and to change direction(based upon the Red Light law).

What do you think was going on in the mind of the manager massaging the new secretary's neck and observing her just sitting there? This man would wait with great anticipation for the next opportunity to approach her again. He would do anything in his power to create a situation in which he could force himself upon her. He saw her as a soft, weak, and easy target. His main goal, in the long run, was to put her in bed.

So, for Jenny, there was no solution in view if she suffered from low self-esteem. This boss would put so much pressure on Jenny that either she would go to bed with him or leave the job.

There are thousands of examples where women suffer from low self-esteem and do not display the courage to do what should be done in certain circumstances involving moments of self-debate. The modern woman in our society must understand that she must be very aggressive in such cases. **She must not let the situation go out of control so that later on it is impossible to stop the process.** The woman is the only one who will end up paying the dues.

If Jenny would have stopped the moment she should have stopped, this manager would have accepted the message immediately and ceased his behavior. In his mind, he would put her in a place where she deserved respect. He would understand not to fool around with this new secretary, at least not without her permission.

When the issue of "man/child" was previously discussed, it was emphasized that **men do not understand indirect messages, speech, reactions, or actions.** Men understand only direct, clear methods of communication at every level. They appreciate firm and polite aggressive behavior. **Respect is given by them to women who stay in control and not to women who behave in a subservient manner.** The moment that Jenny froze on her seat from fear, the man translated that Jenny agreed to his actions and was enjoying them. In his mind: **She agreed to his actions because she did not say anything and she did not do anything. Therefore, she must be enjoying them.**

The same situation that happened to Jenny in the workplace exists in many other relationships between men and women. Many times the man puts the woman down by humiliating and abusing her verbally or even physically. At other times, he may make up for this behavior by making her feel good or making apologies. Then, the next moment he is abusing her again.

For some reason, the woman continues with this see-saw type of relationship, always trying to solve the problem she is in with partial solutions that will never bring the right answer to her problem. **A woman should be in complete control of the relationship.** That is why it is not healthy and not normal when the woman is controlled by a man who is humiliating and abusing her.

Such a woman must stop the process immediately without hesitation, simply because a partial solution is not a serious solution to the problem. Any serious solution requires permanency. The permanent solution is to stop any bad relationship, any humiliation or abuse, and to change direction. **GET OUT AND STAY OUT.**

****

CHAPTER FIFTEEN: STRIP-TEASE

Many men like to visit nude clubs for various reasons. The main reason is lack of sexual satisfaction due to unfulfilled fantasies.

It has been mentioned previously in this book that men have many desires and dreams of a sexual nature based upon their individual weaknesses, which if unfulfilled by the woman, will lead to frustration and the desire for fulfillment outside of the relationship. Going to a nude club places men in a high state of arousal as **their fantasies come to life.**

This state of arousal can lead to two end results. The man may go back home to his woman with all these pictures in his mind and make love to her with great gusto. Although she may enjoy the moment, this man is not really making love to her. It is the stripper who fulfilled his fantasies. The danger exists that if this state of affairs should continue, a situation will arise with the second end result.

The second situation reveals the man utilizing the "extra services" that some of these clubs provide. In this case the man is fulfilling his fantasy with the object of his fantasy directly.

Basically, if a man has the constant desire to visit nude clubs, this presents a Red Light situation. To remind you, **when you see a red light you must stop and change direction.** The woman must either fulfill the man's fantasies or leave the relationship.

If a woman really cares about her man and feels that he is basically a good man, then she should try to fulfill his fantasies as best she can. In this case, she will be doing things that he likes in order to control him. She needs to create fantasy dramas complete with costume in order to entice him and excite him. If the bedroom decor does not provide any sexual stimulation, then she should redecorate in such a way as to provide a new and exciting atmosphere.

For example, the woman might line her bedroom walls with mirrors so that the man might view the woman's body part he covets during the course of lovemaking. She might purchase a four-poster bed and decorate it with filmy curtains and soft, sensual materials to create a scene out of India or the Middle East, complete with hot and exciting colors. If the man's fantasies are still back in the 60's, she might put mattresses on the floor covered with Indian spreads, place beaded curtains around the room along with psychedelic artwork, and burn incense constantly. The key is to use your imagination.

However, the best solution is not to wait until you find out that your man has gone elsewhere to fulfill his fantasies. From the beginning of the relationship, develop fantasies for him based upon his particular weakness and act upon these fantasies. **This creates the best control.**

Now, let us return back to the nude club and understand what really happened there.

One woman is exposing herself in front of a large group of men. What she is doing is playing with them and controlling them as she wants. In some clubs, the strippers even go down amongst the tables and sit astride the men's knees. The rules are very clear. The men are not allowed to touch the strippers. Yet, the strippers go as far as they want with the men up to exposing them. They control the game.

The man knows that he is not allowed to do anything and that the stripper can tease him as much as she desires to. This creates an immense amount of sexual tension.

In such a group of men, you can find very aggressive or abusive men by nature. However, the majority of men in these clubs somehow follow all the rules. They do not do this out of fear of the bouncers or the police. They behave this way because the dancer is creating a body language which clearly states: "I control the situation here. I will push you to a level of excitement wherein you will almost lose your mind. But you will never cross the line." **This is a pure control created by this dancer.**

The only reason for men losing control in some clubs is the loss of control by the dancer. A dancer who is unsure of herself and obviously demonstrates this through her body language and facial expressions will create a situation of chaos.

A woman who reaches this high level of control by doing the same thing that the stripper is doing in the nude club is using her feminine sexuality with such intensity that the man is controlled 100%. It is highly recommended that women who want to see what really happens in these nude clubs purchase videos that show the behavior of men in this situation. A woman can learn a lot about men's behavior in this environment. Later on, after gaining this knowledge, she can utilize the information for her personal gain.

To remind you again, as has been stated throughout this book, **the most powerful force that a woman has to control her man is her sexuality.** Following this are all her other qualities.

Let us look at an imaginary classroom where a beautiful and sexy teacher dressed in a long, loose skirt is attempting to teach mathematics to a group of men. The concepts are very boring, and the teacher places many formulas on the board along with examples of problems. The men are having trouble paying attention and retaining information. They feel frustrated as they observe the teacher, and they cannot concentrate. On the one hand, the teacher is very sexy but, on the other hand, she is attempting to impart very dry material. The men feel that something is wrong.

Now, let us imagine that this teacher suddenly removes all her clothing and sits on the lap of one of the men, promising that he will be allowed to touch her buttocks if he can recite the formulas and complete the problem on the board. She then tells the remainder of the group that they will also be allowed to touch her if they do the same. These men will suddenly be very motivated to learn this math as quickly as possible.

This example may seem quite bizarre, but it represents an analogy to many situations in life. In order to control a man, you must give him instant rewards of your sexuality. **Whenever you want something from him, give him something.**

****

CHAPTER SIXTEEN: THE LAST TANGO

SENSE OF SMELL

Within the brain of every man still exist cells going back to the time of the cave man. As with the animals of our world, many men are sensitive to the smell of a female in heat. This   smell is an odor produced by the vagina when a female is hot or ready for sex. Many women do not feel comfortable with this odor and try to conceal it with the many products available on the market today.

When some men gain wind of this particular odor they become sexually aroused. This group of men belong to the group we have mentioned before that we may call the "animal men". The animal desire is very strong in their system as they have a close affinity to the nature of animals.

Relating these men to our four groups of body type preferences, we can place these men in Group A(The Breast Men) and Group B(The Buttocks Men). There are few men who do not enjoy this female smell and they are, of course, far less animalistic in nature. Removed from what is natural, they are happy with those products that conceal the special odors produced by the female. These men can be placed in Group C(The Leg Men) and Group D(The Face Men).

A smart woman whose man is a Group A or Group B man can save a lot of money by avoiding these products of concealment available on the market. On the other hand, she can supply her man with the exciting "natural" smell that will put her man in such a state of arousal that she will ultimately receive the utmost satisfaction. He will be like the moose in Alaska who, after glorifying in a female scent, is ready to do anything to satisfy the female.

Due to many of the problems posed by modern life, a great deal of men suffer from lack of desire for sex. Although the natural female smell should be able to bring most men out of this state, instead a majority of women exacerbate the problem through use of products which conceal that sexual femininity.

It is the woman's responsibility to discover to what group her man belongs and to then behave accordingly to bring out the best in him. This, in turn, will serve to give the woman greater satisfaction and control of her man.

WHAT YOU REALLY MEAN WHEN YOU SAY NO

In most cases in which a woman is saying "NO" to a man, it sounds like "YES". Every "NO" with a half-smile, every "NO" with a low voice, every "NO" that is not firm, every "NO" with a question mark, every "NO" with eyes looking downward is a "YES" in the eyes of a man.

If you really stand behind your "NO", you have to express it in the opposite manner of all the "NO's" above. It should sound like **"NO!"**

MODESTY

Often when going out on a first date with a man, the woman might find him very attractive and be anxious for physical closeness, even though the man might be stand-offish. She might wonder why he is not making advances towards her and feel, perhaps, that a little assertiveness on her part might do the trick. Maybe he is shy or preoccupied and needs a little awakening.

When it is time to say goodnight at the door, the woman might feel as though she should offer her lips for a kiss, or lightly plant a kiss on the man's cheek. **No good! Do not do this!**

If the woman does this, she immediately loses a portion of respect in the eyes of the man. The man expects to be the aggressor on the one hand and, on the other hand, expects the woman to project naivete and lack of experience. He likes to take the lead and feel that he is in control.

A smart woman will play the game and allow him to take the lead, at which point she will then be able to exert her positive control. We again recommend a viewing of the movie "Kama Sutra" to illustrate this point. In this film, the women initially play a cat and mouse game with the men, even though they have extensive experience, and gradually bring the men into their control.

INFLUENCE OF THE MEDIA

In our lives we see and hear so much negativity in films, television, magazines, newspapers, and radio. We are left with the feeling that all people are bad and there is no longer any good in the world. Unfortunately, the media brings negative events to our attention since it is these events that garner our attention and bring the advertising dollars in.

All this negativity creates a "brainwash" effect in the minds of people. Women claim that "there are no good men out there" and men claim that "there are no good women out there". They convince themselves that this is the reality, and women do not search for the "good men", accepting the Red Light men or the men from the 99% group. This way of thinking is a self-destructive way of thinking.

If we actually examine the number of cases presented negatively by the media and compare this to the population, we can see that there really are very many good people out there. Be positive and be aware of the trap of negativity. Be smart.

SEXUAL LIBERATION

Many men are unable to perform well in bed due to barriers they hold inside themselves. These barriers can come from events in childhood, problems in the past with women, fear, sexual problems, etc. **It is very important to release the man from his problems so that he can perform well, which, in turn, can bring the woman to a better control and put him in a very happy mood.**

In many cases it is difficult to tell if a man is suffering from such barriers. It is the woman's position to determine if any barriers exist and to release him from these in order to control him.

The best test to determine if a man is liberated or not is to encourage him to masturbate and reach orgasm while being observed by the woman next to him. If the man is unable to do this, it is the woman's job to ever so slowly bring him to the situation where he is able to do so. She should masturbate herself in front of him while encouraging him to do the same. **This show of liberation on the part of the woman will excite and entice the man to free himself.**

The man who is unable to reach orgasm while having oral sex performed by the woman is also in need of liberation. The same curative as mentioned above applies in this case as well.

RESTLESSNESS

Have you often observed the relationship of men to their television remote controls? Once one of these is in the hand of a man, it appears that he is constantly surfing the channels, impatient to find the program he is interested in and not waiting long enough for a commercial to end so that he might see what program is on that particular channel. He constantly flicks back and forth, from station to station. As soon as a commercial begins, he is surfing again. If there is a dull moment in the program he is watching, again back to the remote control.

Why is man so impatient, restless, and unfocused? From where do these characteristics come? The answer lies in the **sexual behavior of man.**

The majority of men still carry with them the sexual instincts of animal nature. In nature, animals are surrounded by so many enemies that there is no time for anything but a brief interlude of sex. This was also the case for early man. Sex was a very fast act, since man had many natural enemies about as well as other men who were interested in taking his woman away. He had to ensure the survival of his genes.

If you watch *The Discovery Channel* on your television, you may observe such behavior throughout the animal kingdom. There are even special programs shown occasionally which focus exclusively on the sexual behavior of animals.

Observing our "cousins" - the monkeys - in the wild, you see widespread evidence of this behavior in these very active animals. The sexual act involves a quick performance by the male, no matter how hot the female may be.

Now, if we return to humankind, we may see a similar behavior in the primitive tribes of our world today. The male goes directly to the point. There are very few preliminaries to the sexual act. Although this may seem very strange, the women accept this behavior as natural. Even in the modern world, this practice remains in effect among several religious groups.

As technology has advanced through time, women, through the additional freedoms they have gained, have sought more pleasures for themselves. Men, in order to obtain women, have adjusted to their desires. They have learned to provide preliminaries to lovemaking to include wining and dining as well as kissing and caressing. These preliminaries, mind you, are all the ideas of women.

Let's consider the issue of wining and dining and its relationship to the sexual behavior of men. If we again go back to nature, we can see that the animals eat quickly and ravenously, anxious to retain the food for their own use and to avoid being an easy target for their enemies. This, again, was also the practice of early man and these habits are still ingrained in the subconsciousness of present day man. A group of men in a campground, on an expedition, or in the army will just grab their food and eat it quickly without any conversation or fanfare, not caring how or what it is served on.

So, it is evident that the whole idea of fine dining was invented by women, who enjoy social discourse, beauty in their surroundings, and fine details - things that make this world a better place. Entire industries grew up around this idea as women became more creative in their efforts to beautify the home and create a pleasant social atmosphere.

Modern man is now in the situation where he has learned to enjoy many of these accessories and arrangements, yet he can just as readily do without them. Most modern women could not adjust well to being without these accessories, social practices, and preliminaries to dining and sex.

A good example of this would be a situation involving the pilot of a small airplane making an emergency landing in the deep jungle of the Amazon River. Disembarking from the plane, the pilot finds himself surrounded by a local tribe of friendly nature inviting him to the camp as a member of the tribe. Lacking a working radio or any other form of communication, destiny has determined the path his life is to follow.

Should this pilot be a man, he would readily assimilate into the culture of this primitive tribe. Eating quickly with his hands from a communal bowl would be like second nature to him. In the evening, or as the urge dictates, he would not find it a problem at all to quickly perform sex with his given woman without any preliminaries of kissing, cuddling, or caressing. He would do fine without any presentations of gifts to her or special conversation. Speech would not even be a necessary prelude.

On the other hand, should this pilot be a woman, life would become very difficult for her. She would, at first, lose her appetite upon discovering the way she would have to eat, notwithstanding what she might have to eat. Later, when so ravenously hungry that she couldn't stand it anymore, she would have to eat what was offered her, but would find herself suffering silently after the meal and, perhaps, suffering from indigestion. She would also find it difficult to get enough to eat since it would not be natural for her to grab her food from a communal bowl. But, she would learn these practices in time as necessary to survival.

What she would find even more difficult to accept would be her new sexual role in this tribe. Given to a man not of her choosing, she would be subjected to his sexual desires at his whim without the advantage of any preliminaries or niceties. She would have to accept this or be dismissed from the tribe and lose her only method of survival. She would feel as though she were constantly abused, savagely ravaged, and thrown about like a toy. This would be intolerable for her, and she would probably never adjust.

Although these major differences exist between men and women, it is the control of the woman that puts them on a parallel course with her end benefit in view.

THE SINS OF THE FATHER ARE VISITED UPON THE SON**

Before getting involved in a serious relationship, a woman should make sure that she meets the parents of the man she is interested in. The behavior of the parents themselves, as well as the interaction between the parents and son is a great indicator as to the outcome of the potential relationship between you and your man.

If a woman sees any red lights in the behavior of the parents, she can expect that this behavior may later show up as a red light in the behavior of her man. And, if she sees any red lights in the behavior of her man towards his parents, she can expect that this behavior will later become a problem between her and her man.

Another strong indicator is the behavior of the man's father towards the mother. This is a behavior that has been ingrained in your man since early childhood. Even if it is not showing up at this point, you can bet that there is a good chance that it will show up later in the relationship. This is a red light.

If you should have children old enough to be involved in a relationship, and you have the good fortune of an open and loving relationship with them, it is highly advised that you inform them of the above information.

GIFT TIME

All women like to receive gifts from their men, even when it is not a special occasion. It is an art to know when to pass the suggestion or pose the request.

If it has been some time since you received a gift, and you feel that it is now the time, you need to approach your man in the right way and at the right time.

You are at the shopping mall with your man, with no particular reason in mind. Suddenly you see something that really catches your eye and you feel you can not do without. You know that the price of the item will not give your man a heart attack or put him in bankruptcy. Tell your man that you would like to rest for a bit on one of the benches provided for this purpose in the mall. As you sit next to him, begin to kiss him passionately and whisper in his ear: "Honey, I don't know what has come over me, but suddenly I feel this wave of heat. I want to make love to you. Let's go home immediately." Stay on the bench just long enough, continuing to kiss, until you feel your man is on the edge and about to lose control.

On the way out, stop abruptly by the window displaying the item of your desire, and tell him that you just want to take a second to look at this item. Call him and tell him how much you love this item. Your man will probably try to whisk you away from this item as fast as he can. But you must tell him how badly you want this item.

Your man is so anxious to do anything to get home now, that he will do whatever he has to do to speed up the process and still retain the mood. He will quickly buy the item for you, whisk you out of the store, and stride rapidly out of the mall with you to your car.

Now, you must not forget to give him what you have promised to give him with the fullest passion you are able to provide. Make the experience worth his while. Give him lots of ice cream with hot fudge sauce and candy toppings.

This advice is based upon a combination of sexual tension and control, that women should apply whenever necessary in special circumstances. Remember, to be creative and utilize various approaches to the same goal. No matter the approach, the reward should remain the same.

The trick is to approach your man when he is feeling well and in the right frame of mind. Starting at this point, you can begin to apply the sexual tension and control.

USING THE WORD "LOVE" TO OBTAIN SEX"

There is a phenomena existing in the relationship between a young virgin girl and a young man. The young man is very anxious to have sex, and he puts a great deal of pressure on the young woman who is reluctant to give up her virginity. The young male will use many different techniques to achieve his goal.

The most common technique is to verbalize his unendurable discomfort in the genital region. He states to the girl: "Because I cannot have sex I suffer from a terrible pain in my scrotum. This pain is very unhealthy, and I heard that later in life this can cause a cancer of the scrotum. If you really love me, you will understand this and agree to have sex with me. But if you cannot understand my point, then I will have to seek a solution elsewhere, as my health is most important."

A smart girl will give a very short and accurate answer to such a young man. She will tell him: "Honey, if you really loved me, you would never push me in that direction. If you think it is necessary to leave me because I will not have sex with you, then you do not really love me. God bless you and your inflamed scrotum."

VARIATIONS IN TASTE AMONG MEN

Most men from the Middle East or Latin countries(basically hot areas of the world) prefer women with extra meat. In most cases, they like this meat to be distributed in the areas of the buttocks and thighs. A cushy, soft, but well-formed rear is a delight to them. Women possessing such attributes hold a far higher value in their eyes and are far preferred over the so-called "perfect women"(model types). Conclusively, women with extra meat appear as strong sex objects to men from these areas.

Sometimes, in cold climates such as Scandanavia, Denmark, or Iceland one can be surprised at finding men with similar tastes. This situation seems to occur as the result of these men having moved from the areas previously mentioned or as the result of genes from these family types passed on to them.

PASSION OVER THE MILES

Your man must be in touch with your essence all the time - the feel of you, the scent of you. When he sees you often, it is not a problem to provide him with these needs. But when life creates circumstances which force a separation for a period of time(for example: business trips, army reserves or training, family emergencies, etc.), it is suggested that you supply these needs through alternative measures.

When a lengthy separation must occur, provide your man with a naked photograph of yourself along with **recently worn underwear containing a strong scent of your natural body fluids.** In addition to these primary items, supply him with an item of lingerie containing the scent of the perfume you wear that he adores so much. A surprise note or cassette tape expressing your passion and love for him, along with suggestive and erotic sounds or words would accessorize the package.

In possession of these sensual reminders of you, your man will think only of you and will not be motivated to look for sensual excitement elsewhere. You may think of this as a form of sexual tension or remote control. No matter how you may categorize this approach, it is a good thing to do.

If your man is uncomfortable with a direct approach, be sure to sneak these items somehow into his suitcase. He will be pleasantly surprised.

HOT WOMEN

Throughout the book the impression may be given that only the men are anxious for sex and that their sex drive is far greater than that of women's. However, there are numerous women with a sex drive so strong that it may equal or supercede that of men.

Such women need to be careful not to make the man feel inferior sexually. In other words, no matter how passionate they may feel, they should restrain from approaching the man too aggressively **early in dating or a relationship.** Later on, when the relationship has developed, the man will probably be very appreciative of such a woman.

It is even easier for a hungry woman to keep her man in control. None of the approaches mentioned previously in this book will be an effort for her. She will lustfully and joyfully utilize the methods to keep her man in control. But, in many cases, she must give him the feeling that he is the aggressor even though, in fact, she is the one. **Remember that soft and quiet waters run deep.**

Often, when a woman is too aggressive early in the relationship, she will scare the man away. At this point, the man likes to feel that he is running the show. And, if you remember the section on Virginity, you may recall that the man will think of such a woman as a slut, and lose all respect for her.

Here we may again bring up the original film titled "Kama Sutra". In this movie, the courtesans were trained to please a man in every way possible. They may be thought of today as high-end callgirls for a specific clientele. These women were very experienced and passionate, yet when summoned by a man of royal standing, they behaved in a coquettish manner, always at first giving the appearance of inexperience until the man began to make some moves. Even at this point, they would proceed in a very slow and soft manner, allowing the man to think that he was taking the lead. This well-taught approach was an art form that every woman should learn.

Therefore, no matter how strong your passion may be, learn to restrain yourself and allow the man to think that he is taking the lead. Try to put a lid on your steam if you can and vent it slowly.

FEAR OF SWEAT

The subconscious mind of the animalistic man is attuned to many outward behaviors of women that give strong clues to their nature and desires. These behaviors are often viewed in areas such as nightclubs, dance clubs, gyms, beaches and swimming pools, etc.

When going to a dance club, for example, and observing women dancing, the animalistic man(who has been discussed in Chapter 10) will immediately be attracted to the women who dance wildly and have **no fear of sweat.** The sweat, in the subconscious mind of this type of man, reminds him of high performance lovemaking involving a lot of activity and, subsequently, a lot of sweat.

Women who must constantly groom themselves to insure the "perfect look", and who cannot tolerate having their makeup disturbed or a hair on their head out of place will not attract this type of man in those areas mentioned above. A woman who does not object to perspiration during activity also comes across as more of a free spirit - a woman not afraid to experiment and have an open attitude towards new ideas. This is also appealing to such a man.

Conversely, a woman searching for a man with the animalistic nature may observe the same behaviors in similar locations. He will also be the man dancing wildly on the dance floor and having no fear of perspiration.

GOOD COOKS, GOOD LOVERS

Since gourmet cooking requires a great deal of patience, imagination, passion, sensitivity, coordination, and fortitude - all characteristics of a good lover - it is easy to surmise that a man who cooks well and with great pleasure will also make love on the same level. Such a man will bring a woman the utmost of satisfaction - great sex and great food.

A man who enjoys cooking will open the door to more situations of shared intimacy, where the joy of cooking is shared by both man and woman. In some situations, the practice of preparing food for a special meal, and then sharing the meal together, may even act as a prelude to sex. You may be presented, in this way, with additional opportunities to create sexual tension and, subsequently, greater control over your man.

The only dangers herein, are the side effects of the cooking process, which requires a great deal of testing by tasting. These dangers are weight gain, lack of desire to exercise due to a full stomach, and the subsequent effect on the bedroom activity.

The method of avoiding these dangers is illustrated in the following subchapter.

EXERCISE/SEXERCISE

At the time of life approaching middle age, both men and women often find that they no longer have the same energy, stamina, or muscle tone that they did in previous years. To compound this problem, they often find many extra pounds have been added to their youthful weight. The lack of muscle tone and the additional weight can also lead to a variety of back problems, particularly in the lower regions. Pain in the lower back has repercussions of an adverse effect on sexual activity.

Any or all of these problems may lead to decreased sexual activity along with less satisfying encounters, combined with a decrease in the amount of the sex hormones normally produced by the body.

Mary, feeling a loss of libido and noticing a decrease in her husband Larry's desire and stamina, decided to read up on the subject, soon discovering that a lack of exercise was at the root of the problem. She decided to do everything she could to encourage Larry to join a gym with her and workout together. Larry was extremely hesitant, complaining that he was too tired to exercise after a long work day, and that he was concerned that he may even have further problems with his aching back. After much coercion, through offers of massage and special TLC, Mary convinced Larry to join the gym.

Before eating dinner, Mary and Larry began to regularly exercise at the gym two nights during the week and one day during the weekend. At first, Mary would reward Larry with a soap massage in the shower, or an oil massage before going to sleep for the night. Before long, Larry began to appreciate the benefits of the exercise on its own merits. Suddenly, he found himself having increased stamina and energy. With the endorphins created through the physical activity still in play upon his return home with Mary, his libido was strong, and he was anxious for a round of "sexercise". Mary, having these same thoughts and feelings, was just as anxious as he was. Suddenly, the passion, and excitement of their youth had appeared with renewed vigour.

Now this "sexercise" created even greater fulfillment in their lives. "Sexercise" is an extremely physical, energetic and lengthy form of lovemaking which, when completed, will not only result in a high level of sexual fulfillment, but also the rewarding feeling of having had a wonderful workout. Therefore, the amount of endorphins released will be multiplied, and the lasting effect of these endorphins will be dependent upon the time spent in making love.

If a really lengthy session takes place, then the endorphins may last strongly for two hours. You and your partner will be in a state of bliss for this time, and the memory of this will be retained for even longer.

So, one of the most important things you can do to assist and enhance the sexual relationship with your man is physical exercise. Exercise will enable "sexercise", and "sexercise" will increase the desire for more exercise, since the benefits of that exercise will have been realized. There is no greater cycle to establish.

THE KEY TO SUCCESS

POSITIVE CONTROL

THROUGH SEXUAL

TENSION

EPITOME

If you only knew how to play with me wisely.
If you only knew how to rule me with a gentle hand.
If you only knew how to play this ancient game of wisdom,
That only a few women understand.

I would freely change to be your slave.
I would change to be your good and proper man.
I would stay by your side eternally,
And bow to your delicate, good authority,
Your mastery of pleasure and satisfaction,
Your benevolent, gentle strength.

If you only knew how to play this game with me,
I would be your slave forever.

--Harrison Forrest

****

ATTN: LADIES, ENCLOSED IS A NEW SERVICE CALLED

Personal Advice on a Cassette Tape

TO RECEIVE PERSONAL ADVICE FROM HARRISON FORREST: (A) *PLEASE PRINT ONLY 2 PAGES* OF YOUR CASE (PROBLEM). (SORRY WE CAN'T ACCEPT HANDWRITING).
PLEASE PRINT YOUR NAME & ADDRESS CLEARLY

(B)PLEASE SEND CHECK IN THE AMOUNT OF $59.00 TO:
SABRA INT'L C/O AMINGWAY PUBLISHING
POST OFFICE BOX 770546
CORAL SPRINGS, FL 33077
PH:954-346-8588 FAX:954-346-6762
E-MAIL:sabra-tifferent-53@worldnet.att.net

(C) *YOU WILL RECEIVE A PERSONAL CASSETTE TAPE ANSWERING YOUR OWN PERSONAL CASE, DIRECT FROM MR.HARRISON.*

BECAUSE OF A HIGH VOLUME OF RESPONSE, PLEASE ALLOW 3 TO 5 WEEKS.

SEMINARS BY HARRISON FORREST:

DEAR LADIES, AT THIS POINT, WE PROVIDE SEMINARS IN THE SOUTH FLORIDA AREA. HOWEVER THERE ARE SPECIAL ARRANGEMENTS AVAILABLE FOR ORGANIZED GROUPS OF WOMEN _ALL OVER THE U.S.A. (DEPENDENT ON THE SIZE OF THE GROUP)._

FOR MORE INFORMATION ABOUT HARRISON'S SEMINARS

PLEASE MAIL YOUR REQUEST TO:
HARRISON FORREST
POST OFFICE BOX 770546
CORAL SPRINGS, FL 33077

PLEASE PRINT YOUR NAME AND ADDRESS CLEARLY

ORDER FORM
TO ORDER PLEASE MAIL,FAX, OR E-MAIL TO:

SABRA INT'L C/O AMINGWAY PUBLISHING
POST OFFICE BOX 770546
CORAL SPRINGS, FL 33077
PH:954-346-8588 FAX:954-346-6762
e-mail:sabra-tifferent-53@worldnet.att.net

PLEASE SEND THE FOLLOWING BOOKS:

see cost on the back of the book: 1)_____.

2)_____ 3)_____

amount of books:_____price:_____total:_____

BOOKS CAN BE RETURNED FOR A FULL REFUND. BOOKS MUST BE IN
PERFECT CONDITION. RETURNS MUST BE MADE WITHIN 15 DAYS OF
RECEIVING TIME.

We accept:personal checks, mony orders, credit cards,
& company checks.(sorry no c.o.d.)

sales tax: Florida res. add 6%_____.

shipping in the U.S.A.$3.95 for the first book & $2.00 for each
additional book. _____

T O T A L:_____

print clearly
name:_____

address:_____

city:_____state:_____zip:_____

we accept:Visa// Master Card//Amex//Discover

card #_____exp date____/____/____

name on card_____signature_____

DISCOUNT ON QUANTITY

ORDER FORM
TO ORDER PLEASE MAIL,FAX, OR E-MAIL TO:

SABRA IN'L C/O AMINGWAY PUBLISHING
POST OFFICE BOX 770546
PH:954-346-8588 FAX:954-346-6762
CORAL SPRINGS, FL 33077
e-mail:sabra-tifferent-53@worldnet.att.net

PLEASE SEND THE FOLLOWING BOOKS:

see cost on the back of the book: 1)_____.

2)_____ 3)_____

amount of books:_____price:_____total:_____

BOOKS CAN BE RETURNED FOR A FULL REFUND. <u>BOOKS MUST BE IN PERFECT CONDITION</u>. RETURNS MUST BE MADE WITHIN 15 DAYS OF RECEIVING TIME. (U.S. POST OFFICE RETURN RECEIPT IS REQUESTED)

We accept:personal checks, money orders, credit cards, & company checks.(sorry no c.o.d.)

<u>sales tax</u>: Florida res. add 6%_____.

<u>shipping</u> in the U.S.A.$3.95 for the first book & $2.00 for each additional book. _____

T O T A L:_____

print clearly
name:_____

address:_____

city:_____state:_____zip:_____

we accept:<u>Visa</u>// <u>Master Card</u>//<u>Amex</u>//<u>Discover</u>

card #_____exp date____/___/____

name on card_____signature_____

D I S C O U N T   O N   Q U A N T I T Y